The Interview Chain

Lynn Farley-Rose

www.hhousebooks.com

Paperback ISBN: 978-1-910688-58-8

Cover design by Jo Dalton
Typeset by Polgarus Studio

Published in the UK

Holland House Books
Holland House
47 Greenham Road
Newbury, Berkshire RG14 7HY
United Kingdom

www.hhousebooks.com

We've got a budget deficit that's important, we've got a trade deficit that's critical, but what I worry about most is our empathy deficit. When I speak to students, I tell them that one of the most important things we can do is to look through somebody else's eyes.

Barack Obama

Contents

Introduction

Ideas often come when you're not expecting them and that's just what happened with *The Interview Chain*. It showed up one winter morning as I stood on the platform of my local station gazing idly at the London-bound commuters on what was turning out to be the first properly chilly day of the year. As they hunched against the drizzle, most of them communed with their phones and a small minority stared vacantly across the track. Here and there, pointy-toed shoes or a bright scarf introduced a touch of drama to the sober woollen coats and beige macs. But despite being such a diverse collection of individuals, no one person stood out—there was nothing overtly remarkable about *any* of them.

It's precisely because railway stations and trains are for the most part predictable places that they provide such seductive material for fiction writers. While solitary travellers sink into temporary private bubbles, and snippets of humdrum conversation pass in and out of focus, things may appear mundane. And yet there's an ever-present tension between the seen and the unseen and the lives of our fellow travellers may in reality prove to be anything but ordinary. The poet John Koenig came up with the word *sonder* to describe the realisation that each random passerby has a life that's as vivid and complex as our own.

I stared at a young woman with streaked cyan hair, at a man with a shaved head and an older woman clutching her suitcase handle for support. What mattered to them? What shaped them? What were they proud of? Had they lived enough to have regrets?

I shifted up a gear and started to think about the population of the world and the fact that my fellow travellers were an infinitesimal percentage of the seven billion individuals alive that day. Seven *billion*—that's a lot of lives. A lot of stories.

Real life stories have that extra ingredient that fiction can never have. Escaping into made-up stories and beautiful prose is one kind of pleasure, but watching a film based on fact prompts us to empathise and explore how we ourselves would react in a similar situation. Radio programmes like Desert Island Discs, Last Word, and The Listening Project are popular because they're about real people's lives, and are therefore always original and unpredictable. They're amongst my own favourite listening material and I'd recently been thinking about collecting a few stories myself for a blog I was writing. It needed regular fuel so I was constantly on the lookout for ideas, especially anything that caused me to step outside my own life and talk to people who could show me a different view of the world.

Only a few months before I'd met someone who did exactly that. It happened when I stayed as an Airbnb guest in a small modern house in Delft while travelling on my own in Holland. The owner had many five-star reviews and as I made a cup of tea in his kitchen and nibbled on a stroopwafel we got chatting. He gave me lots of useful information about the local area, and the next evening he invited me to share the food he'd cooked—a fragrant Iraqi dish of spiced vegetables and rice. We sat at his table, eating and swapping life stories. He listened attentively to my contributions and asked interested questions, but I had nothing to say that could compare with the dramas he'd experienced and which he recounted so vividly that I could see them as if I was watching a film. I learned that he had grown up in a moderately affluent family in Baghdad. "Iraq was a clean and beautiful country," he said with pride. "It had many cultured people and there was a great respect for books. But then the war came and that changed everything. My father was killed and I knew that my life was in danger, too." He fled Baghdad and a Kurdish family friend helped him escape across the border to Turkey where he got a job as a waiter in a pizza restaurant in Istanbul. For eighteen months he worked fifteen-hour days, seven-day weeks, and slept on a wet basement floor with other illegal immigrants. Eventually, he had enough money to get a fake passport and after a terrifying journey he made it to the Netherlands. When he arrived at Amsterdam airport he sat for hours in the arrivals area, alone and afraid as he tried to pluck up the courage to identify himself as an asylum seeker. After that came many months in detention centres and countless interrogations, but in the end he was granted Dutch citizenship. Twenty-six years later, the man I met was a hard-working professional, a perfect host, and a devoted father to his little daughter. Before that evening, I'd been sympathetic to refugees and asylum seekers but once I'd been affected by this man's story their plight was no longer an abstract notion. I could no longer be blind, could no longer claim ignorance. That was a conversation that changed me.

As I stood on the platform shivering and daydreaming, my brain gradually began to do some joined-up thinking. I'd been nosily speculating about my fellow travellers in foreground mode, and hadn't even been aware that it was gnawing away at the blog problem in background mode. My train arrived and I settled into the dusty carriage with the beginnings of an idea.

I could do a series of interviews for my blog. The problem was that while I believe that everyone has something interesting to say if you take the time to listen and ask questions, I knew that I was after something more than that; I wanted a supply of surprising and inspiring stories. Then I thought of a twist. I would ask each interviewee to pass me on to someone they admire. That was almost guaranteed to unearth some thought-provoking stories. It would also be intriguing to explore *what* people admire? Out of the hordes of individuals they will have come across in their life why choose *that* one? I guessed that qualities like compassion, wisdom, bravery, and professionalism would crop up and I, for one, would welcome some positive stories as an antidote to the ubiquitous *world gone bad* ones.

By the time I reached the end of my journey two stops down the line, I'd decided to go ahead with what I was now calling the *Chain Interview Project* as if it were an old friend. I was hoping that its personality would turn out to be interesting, inspiring, connected, informative, and thought-provoking. And if it helped to increase empathy then that would be even better. But none of that could happen until I'd decided where to start. Who was going to be my first interviewee?

I decided that it would have to be someone I did not already know. That way I was more likely to be led across unfamiliar territory. I had no idea what kind of person would fit this vague description, but over the following months my antennae were directed towards everyone I encountered and I felt confident that when I met the right person, I would know. During this time I chatted keenly to lots of likely candidates without revealing my ulterior motive. At the same time I tried my best not to come across as intrusive or peculiar, although I'm not sure how well I managed that. The upshot was that I had plenty of pleasant conversations but none that grabbed me in the way I wanted.

It took until the following summer to make a breakthrough. I was invited to a cousin's thirtieth birthday party aboard a Thames cruiser and it was jam-packed with interesting people. At one stage I thought that a sports journalist might be *the one* but in the end I wasn't interested enough in sport to dive in and ask him.

Then, as we were on our way back up the river from Greenwich, I sat outside on deck chatting to a young woman whose strong values and unusual creative ideas were intriguing. I was curious to know more and felt she had the magic ingredient I'd been searching for so I plunged in, explaining about the project, and asking if she would agree to be my first link. It was growing dark and most of the light came from the brightly illuminated buildings along the bank and the multicoloured reflections on the water, so I couldn't see very well. But I could tell enough to know that she was friendly, if a little guarded. And who wouldn't be when the garrulous middle-aged woman they're chitchatting with asks out of the blue if they'd agree to take it to another level and do an interview. Fortunately, I had my cousin on hand to vouch for me so with a cautious smile my first interviewee, Kirsti, gave me her email address and we arranged to meet a few weeks later.

That was how the chain started and Kirsti did not disappoint. After our meeting she passed me on to Megan, and over the next four years, new links were added and the chain grew steadily longer and covered a diverse range of topics. It was a simple model, but one key principle was that although I'd selected the first acorn and planted it, I wanted to let the chain develop organically from then on with minimal intervention on my part. So when interviewees asked me what kind of person they should pass me on to, I deflected the question and asked them to decide.

The first interviews appeared in my blog as intended but as the chain grew and spread across continents I decided to gather them into a book. I wanted this chain of stories to be a physical entity that I could hold, and I looked forward to turning the pages and watching each person's experiences morph into the next.

I was always excited, as each handover approached, wondering who I would meet next and what we would talk about. And now that the chain has twenty links—a nice round number at which to wind things up—I can look back over it and feel glad to have ended up with this particular chain. All of the interviewees took part wholeheartedly and exceeded my hopes for finding interesting, inspiring and surprising stories. They taught me so much and I hate to imagine missing out on talking to *any* of them. But I'm also aware that had any of the interviewees made a different choice about who to pass me on to, then that other chain would no doubt have been satisfying, too. The thing is that we're surrounded by an inexhaustible supply of human stories. No two lives are ever the same. You can be sure that if you ask anyone about their life they will tell you something that makes you see the world differently. Sometimes it's a small insight into something you've never experienced yourself, and occasionally you'll have a lightbulb moment that you'll never forget. Whether big or small, these insights are worthwhile—they build understanding of our human world. They help to make it a kinder and more connected place.

Kirsti

"I arranged for a giant banqueting table to be built... there was an Alice in Wonderland feel to it..."

It's now about nine months since I first had the idea for this project and the only thing I've collected so far is a brief conversation on a riverboat. But today that's all about to change. It's a stiflingly hot day in August and I'm on the train to Waterloo. I've arranged to meet Kirsti in the café at the Royal Festival Hall and I'm so concerned not to be late that I arrive an hour early. Normally I'd welcome the chance to sit with a coffee and gather my thoughts as I watch the restless Thames through the huge windows. But today it's me that's restless and I'm too unsettled to sit down. The project is about to start in earnest and I've never done anything quite like this before. Talking to strangers is not something that we English find easy.

I'm expecting to spend around an hour with Kirsti and during this time I will find out if I can make my idea work. Will I ask the right questions? Will she be prepared to answer them? And then of course there's the question of who she will pass me on to. Will they be willing to talk to me... and so it goes on with self-doubt finding an opportunistic chink and giving me last-minute nerves.

Thankfully Kirsti arrives on time. As the project is so new I've given her very little information about what to expect and I wonder if she might be a bit nervous, too. If we were to meet in either her house or mine, we would no doubt cover any initial awkwardness with the ritualised distraction of putting the kettle on. But here, as it's lunchtime we join a slow queue for food and as we shuffle along we have a preliminary chat, picking up roughly where we left off on the boat. Then armed with trays of salad we jostle our way to a relatively quiet corner and settle down to talk. Once we get going it's much easier than I expected. Kirsti tells me about her life as an artist and how she finds innovative ways to communicate powerful messages. She introduces me to a Healing Giant, community lantern processions, an Incredible Edible Tea Party and other fantastical creations. I learn about her unconventional childhood and deep roots in Wales and I learn too, why she values feeling like an outsider. The time passes quickly and by the end there is, of course, still plenty more I could ask. There always will be but for now I've achieved what I set out to do. I understand where Kirsti came from and how she got to her life today.

How would you describe your work, Kirsti?

It's difficult to say exactly what I do. On my invoices I put *community arts and environmental education* but I think that sounds a bit boring and it doesn't really represent how excited I feel about my projects. I suppose what underpins my work is using art to communicate messages, particularly about climate change and other environmental issues. Those are things that I've been passionate about for a long time.

Can you tell me about your projects at Kew Gardens?

The most recent one has been to do with spices and how they've influenced our world in so many ways. Lots of spices grow in countries where there are rickshaws, and so I came up with the idea of having storytellers take people on personal rickshaw tours for twenty minutes—they get to see some of Kew Gardens and we tell them stories about the spices we pass. So they might see a cinnamon tree, for example, and then get the chance to taste, smell and feel other spice plants.

One of the things we talk about is the history of pepper trading. This made the Venetians incredibly rich. A peppercorn rent now means a nominal amount but there was a time when peppercorns were ridiculously expensive, and you could use a small bag of them to buy a mansion in London. But my favourite spice is probably cardamom. It's used in many different cuisines throughout the world and used to be so precious that Indian royal families would give one another a single cardamom pod in a solid gold box as a present when they came to visit. I don't know what they'd do with it. Smell it? Look at it? Stroke it? Keep it on the mantelpiece? Nowadays we can buy a kilo for fifteen quid.

Another theme I worked on at Kew Gardens was medicinal plants. So I built a raised bed in the shape of a giant human body, and we put in plants with either historical or current medicinal uses for each part of the body. You could wander round the edge and there were lots of interactive things that you could smell, touch, read, or bash, to learn more. It was called *The Healing Giant.*

My first Kew project was *The Incredible Edible Tea Party* and the theme was edible plants. I arranged for a giant banqueting table to be built and it was placed in the middle of a long avenue with huge oak chairs all around. I got my Welsh carpenter friend, Giles, to make it and there was an Alice in Wonderland feel to it. It was big enough to seat forty people and had various plants growing out of the middle. They were planted in hidden trays underneath and were themed round the kinds of things you might eat at a tea party—raspberry jam, piccalilli, salad and other weird but nice things. We got lots of white china and fired patterns on to it, which we got from the Kew illustrations archive and we also carved messages into the pots and the table. It brought people together and captured their imagination. The table is still there and people use it for picnics and birthday treats.

I know that you had quite an unusual childhood…

I grew up at Machynlleth in deepest, darkest Mid Wales. It's an incredibly beautiful place and my parents were part of the influx that set up the Centre for Alternative Technology (CAT) in the '70s and '80s. They were basically just a load of hippies who decided to take over a slate quarry and experiment with renewable energy. But it turned into a really influential project and attracted people from all over the world. There were always plenty of interesting people to talk to and so I feel like I've been part of a movement all my life.

The mix of people was quite strange when I was growing up—there were the people at the Centre, the Welsh sheep farming community, and then there were the other Welsh people who lived locally. We were all nestled together in this tight community.

I was in the first generation of children to grow up at CAT and I went to school locally, so I have lots of Welsh friends and deep roots in that community. I feel a strong connection to Wales and the Welsh, but I have a lot of hippie alternative friends as well, and so in some ways I feel a bit of an outsider. I think that comes from being part of an influx of people in a community that's already well established. That makes you question and value who you are, and creates quite a lot of resilience. It's why I've never felt unsettled by moving around. In fact, I quite enjoy it.

What was your education like?

My secondary school was so small that at one point, I knew the name of everyone who was there. A couple of teachers were inspiring but overall I can't say I really enjoyed it. The emphasis was all on passing exams, and that didn't work so well for me because I was mostly into theatre, music and art. But fortunately I did well in my GCSEs and went on to do performing arts in the sixth form. That was when I got the bug for community arts and so I applied to do a degree in that at the Liverpool Institute for Performing Arts, specialising in drama. One thing I particularly enjoyed was creating lantern processions. The idea is to work with a group of people, maybe even an entire town, and to build lanterns with dried willow and tissue paper. Then everyone gathers together to do a procession or performance with all the lanterns lit up. It's about creating a sense of occasion. I'm interested in celebrating traditions that are very visual, and I like creating new ones.

Birth, marriage and death are big events but generally we've lost a lot of the songs and the support we give to one another. The community where I grew up was different. It was a creative place with lots of these things going on. I really value them and they give people a sense of belonging. That's the biggest thing I've struggled with in London—that you can live next door to someone for five years and not know about their life, whereas in Machynlleth you know everyone on your street and you share such a lot.

I know that after this, you're off to a festival to do some visual minuting. What's that?

I literally bumped into it at a conference at the Centre for Alternative Technology. There was a guy there called Tim Casswell and as people talked, he drew what they were saying. I'd never seen this before but thought it was an incredible technique as I'm a visual learner. In fact, I was so wowed that I joined Tim's merry band and we started working together.

Visual minutes can be done in any kind of meeting. We use huge sheets of architectural paper—typically about two metres tall and ten metres wide. While the speaker is talking, we listen carefully and have to pick up on the essential stuff. Then we think about how to represent the ideas and draw them very fast by hand. It's really fun as you can draw as big as you like and it's all live. There might be a few hundred people watching as you draw. When it's finished it helps people to remember what's been talked about and to understand it better. And sometimes it looks quite beautiful, too.

The first time I saw visual minuting, people were talking about their lives over the past thirty years. Those things are easy to draw but sometimes you get a speaker who's talking about a technical strategy, for example, and as I know nothing about that sort of thing, then I have to try and visualise it. That's where the creativity comes in. I might draw a pattern to represent a network and make it look colourful. It doesn't matter that it's not specified in a technical way. I used to be unsure of what I was doing because it's so hard. But Tim was really encouraging and now I have a stockpile of images that I can draw quickly and I'm much more confident. I've worked with lots of different organisations both big and small, but these days I'm quite choosy about what I do. I don't want to work with organisations that conflict with my values either for environmental reasons or because of the way they treat people. I'm not at all motivated by money.

Tell me about the garden at the Chelsea Flower Show...

I was asked to design it by the Forest Stewardship Council (FSC), an international organisation that promotes sustainable wood production. That includes protecting native forests, setting up replanting programmes, and making sure that people involved in the process are treated well. The FSC gives a seal of approval to timber-based products that meet their criteria.

The Royal Horticultural Society stipulates that all the

products on sale at the Chelsea Flower Show must be from FSC-certified sources and they gave me a space at the show to promote FSC's work. We called it *The Forest in Your Garden* and used it to show how many timber-based products there are in gardens—tool handles, sheds, fences, paths, seed packets, chairs, tables, parasol poles—It also gave people tips on how to incorporate trees into their garden. It won a silver medal and was really fun to do. I worked with some brilliant people.

What's the hardest thing about your work?

It gets nerve wracking when a project comes to an end and I haven't got anything solid to follow it. That's definitely the hardest thing about being self-employed. There's always that worry, and the emotional ebb and flow, particularly as being involved in a project means that I don't have much time to look for the next one. I try to avoid accepting things I don't want to do, simply because I'm panicked but I *am* getting more work these days so that's getting a bit easier.

So, as a self-employed person, how *do* you find work?

It's very much about stumbling around and pulling myself in directions that I find interesting rather than getting into an organisation and working my way up. It's usually been a case of meeting people at the right time and sometimes I've volunteered with organisations that do interesting work so I can see what's going on.

What happened with Kew Gardens was that each summer they invite artists to tender ideas related to that year's theme, and the year I applied the theme was edible plants. I was captivated by the potential it offered and wrote down about five ideas. But there was a blank space at the end of my application, and it looks really bad, doesn't it, when you have more than half a page empty so almost as a way of filling the space, I drew a picture of a giant banqueting table with plants growing out of the middle. I didn't really know how I was going to do it but it filled the space—and of course that was the idea they chose. I had no idea what I was doing when I started so I just made it up.

How optimistic do you feel about our ability to address climate change?

It's something I struggle with as there's a need for optimism in the work I do and if I wasn't optimistic then I'd have given up by now.

I think we may well reach a level of carbon emissions that causes devastating damage to the planet. But I think there will be big technological advances and a swing towards renewable energy for example, which will help to improve things. And the internet has made it much easier for people to get together to work on these things. The environmental movement has shifted from a group of campaigners to a community of people who can actually do something and learn from each other. Those things give me hope.

On the other hand, I also feel pessimistic. The chemistry behind greenhouse gases and climate change is scary and keeps me awake at night. It's a ticking time bomb. And it really does get me that we all know it's happening but we still continue on this course of destruction. I guess, it's quite a big concept for people to accept.

For a long time I've said, "We can do it if people are good

and they care about things other than themselves." Perhaps that's not as true as I'd like it to be. But there *is* still lots of potential. And also once the planet has got rid of us then it will just carry on and form into other things. It's a human experiment really.

Where do you think your work will take you next?

My passions are the environment, bringing people together, and communication, and I love combining them by coming up with ideas and making physical things that get people to understand about climate change and to take some ownership on world issues. I want to do more of that and I've been learning about how to engage people and how they react to information.

I'd also like to do a few more gardens. I really enjoyed Chelsea and although I'm not a horticulturalist it was lovely working with plants so I'm thinking about doing a horticultural or garden design evening course.

August 2015

Megan

"It was my first time at the Climate Change Negotiations and it wasn't a good experience."

I'm on my way to London once again but this time it's a dark and drizzly November evening, quite different from the still, sunny day when I met Kirsti. It's taken longer to get to this second stage than I expected. I'd naively imagined in the beginning that I would move smoothly from one interview to the next with a gap of just a few weeks. But I see now that was unrealistic—people are busy and there are inevitable delays.

I'm looking forward to meeting Megan today. She's a climate change campaigner and researcher, and we've found a brief window between her coming back from the Bonn Climate Change Conference and setting off for the Paris UN Climate Change Conference. Kirsti told me that she chose Megan because she admires 'her energy, passion for justice, and enthusiasm for getting stuck right into issues.' They come from the same part of Wales and their paths have crossed on various projects over the years. These include the time when they took a group of Welsh unemployed youths to Mongolia on the Trans-Siberian Express. I must remember to ask about that.

I meet Megan near London Bridge station and we go to a wine bar. It's full of city workers relaxing loudly at the end of the day and so we have to concentrate hard to hear one another. But if anything the shared discomfort helps to break the ice. Megan's story is not a conventional one of getting a degree and stepping onto an established ladder. She has had to create her own opportunities and her passion for environmentalism has led her from project to project, often working in areas that are suffering the impact of climate change. All this and lots more—and she's still only in her mid-twenties.

Can you take me back to the beginning, Megan. How did you get interested in environmental issues?

Environmentalists often say that they had a 'lightbulb moment' that made them engage and remain engaged but I didn't really have that. For me, it was a gradual process. I think the first thing that happened was when I was sixteen and I had to come up with an idea for a talk at school. My mum had a book on ethical consumerism and I read my way through it and thought it was fascinating. It had all kinds of tables in it, showing, for example, how different brands of jeans compare in terms of ethical production. That kind of data really appealed to me. And it also tied in with realising that I lived in a really beautiful place. My family home is in a harbour in Wales. I spent a lot of time walking our dog and I'd sit and watch the sea. That got me thinking about sustainable development and I got involved in the Welsh Youth Forum for Sustainable Development which was funded by the Welsh Government. We did school assemblies and presentations and put on workshops.

The aim was to raise awareness of climate change amongst young people, and to think about ways to tackle it—like using geothermal energy, for example. We set up a committee and I realised that I had a talent for communicating ideas and organising. I took on more and more responsibility and eventually I became the Chair. I did that for over three years. Lots of interesting opportunities came out of that involvement including going to the UN Climate Change Negotiations in Poland in 2008. It was the first time the UK had sent a youth delegation to the negotiations.

Not only was I one of the youngest there but I was also the only person from Wales. That was important because

Wales is different from the rest of the UK and deserves its own representation. Our culture is based on the land, we have our own music and traditions, and then there's the language—I spoke Welsh at school, I did everything in Welsh. But actually more than anything, I think it's about the people. Welsh people are very friendly. I went to university in Bristol and when I went home, I'd always notice that as soon as the bus took on passengers in Cardiff, the volume would increase dramatically.

It wasn't like I went into the delegation thinking, "I'm representing Wales and I'm going to act very Welsh," but after they started saying things like "Wales is no different from England," then I stood up for us as being part of the UK but having a separate identity too. As soon as you leave a country you're forced to define yourself as who you are and where you're from. I'd never had to think about that before but it was a starting point in defining myself as Welsh.

What happened at the UN Climate Change Negotiations in Poland?

It was my first time at the Climate Change Negotiations and it wasn't a good experience. Before we went, our facilitators had told us that we'd have a lot of influence but there were thousands of people when we got there and it was clear that we couldn't impact the process in any way. That was a learning curve. It taught me that creating expectations that we couldn't meet was disempowering but it didn't put me off engaging with the process—I just felt that in the future we'd have to do things differently.

I spent much of my gap year living in London and gathered together a group of young people who were keen to go to the next UN Climate Change Negotiations which were due to take place the following year in Copenhagen. We all wanted to feel we could make a difference rather than just participating in lobbying, and some of us noticed that many governments send tiny delegations. Typically these are the countries that are *most* affected by climate change, and they are massively underrepresented whereas countries that are less vulnerable to climate change have disproportional representation at the negotiations. But it wasn't just about numbers—it was also about the quality of the involvement.

An example was the leader of the Togo delegation who didn't speak English so unless there was a translator in every room then he couldn't participate. We started UN Fair Play to address the issue of equity in the negotiations. The idea was to make ourselves as useful as possible to the small delegations. Sometimes that involved taking notes in a meeting that they couldn't attend because they only had two delegates and there were five meetings going on at the same time, and other times it was buying them a sandwich. We worked primarily with the delegation from Kiribati—an island in the Pacific that is under threat from rising sea levels. We got a lot of attention because nobody else was addressing this inequity and we worked on it for several years. It needs to be a long-term process and so we produced a report highlighting some of the issues and suggesting solutions. That was well-received.

I know that after that, you went to university in Bristol and got involved in other projects there...

One of the main things was getting involved with FoodCycle. It was an existing charity but they'd never had a node outside London. So I joined some friends in building a node for Bristol. The way it works is that volunteers go out on bikes with trailers and they collect surplus food from outlets like supermarkets—whoever wants to donate, really. Then the volunteers cook a three-course vegetarian meal for people in the community, especially trying to target those suffering from food poverty. We did that in a community centre every Sunday with students doing the transporting and cooking. I was community lead for that first year, so my job was to get people to come along to the meal. We had homeless people, refugees, asylum seekers, travellers, and other people living locally. It was very interesting—we gained a lot of trust because we were there every single week without fail for years, and it's still going.

The next year, I became coordinator and worked with a really good team. The number fluctuated but on average about forty people would come along for the meal. And there was always way too much bread, for example, so people could take that away with them. There was a piano and it was a space to hang out in—we saw people develop. There was this punky, lesbian woman who started out like *nobody touch me* and this homeless guy who just liked to read his newspaper—they became the best of friends. We also did a similar meal for students every two weeks but we charged them for it. That helped the project to be self-sustaining.

Another way of challenging food waste was skipping. My housemates and I did that in a non-official way to get food for our personal consumption and as a result we didn't buy any food for the whole of that year. So, if a freezer broke down at Waitrose, for example, there would be a trailerful of Ben and Jerry's ice cream. We had scallops and lobster—all sorts of things—it was an interesting time. But by the following year, that all changed. I haven't tried for a while so I don't know what it's like now.

At the beginning of my third year at Bristol I went as a delegate to the UNESCO Youth Forum and unfortunately that was a horrible experience. I'd been led to believe that it would be participatory but that turned out to be a lie. The idea was to make the Adult UNESCO Forum look like they were involving young people in decision making when in fact they formulated all the decisions they wanted, ahead of time. There were situations where they'd say, "You guys said that didn't you?" And I would have to say, "No." Many people that came to it just wanted the prestige of being there, having their photo taken with a couple of famous people, and getting the certificate that said they'd participated in a fully democratic experience. Then they could put it on their personal statements and CVs. I hated all of that. The dominant people there were clearly on their way to becoming diplomats and this was just one more box they had to tick.

I gather that you went to Mongolia by train. What was that about?

The idea started at the UN Climate Negotiations in Copenhagen. I'd fundraised to help a young person from the Global South to attend, and was allocated a young woman from Mongolia. We became great friends and talked about all sorts of things, and as a result she decided to set up something equivalent to the Welsh Youth Forum for Sustainable Development (WYFSD) in Mongolia. I said I'd give her online support in doing that and after working together for about a year, I started to think, "Hang on, why don't we take a group of young people to Mongolia...do some skill sharing...and go there and back on the Trans-Siberian Express?" I thought it was a bit crazy but we managed to get funding from GwirVol which is a Welsh funding pot for projects that connect Wales to the international sphere and promote cultural exchanges. They agreed to give us funding provided that half the young people we took were from the WYFSD and the other half were NEETs (Not in Education, Employment or Training). So that's what we did. Kirsti also worked on that project. It was certainly challenging, and the second I got off the train, I twisted my ankle and couldn't walk properly for the whole time we were there.

What were your impressions of Mongolia?

We spent some time in Ulaanbaatar. It's an interesting city—very built up but on the outskirts there's a growing band of nomads who move because of disruption to their nomadic cycles. Mining is really taking over and that disrupts their ability to graze the land and to make money from it. It's really terrible what's happening to them. Also, they burn coal in their gers (tents) and this creates a lot of smog that pollutes the city. But despite the problems, Mongolia is a fantastic, beautiful country and we went into the countryside and stayed in gers several times.

I also had an interesting experience with one of the team, who was 'NEET' at the time. He came across as a really tough nut but as soon as I twisted my ankle, he offered to carry me.

He did that for a couple of days despite being a little skinny guy and during that time we had to make conversation. He'd been lacking a role in the group before this happened, and this was something he could offer. It was hard for him when I got crutches and didn't need his help any more.

The idea of the trip was to help the Mongolians set up a version of what we were doing in Wales. Our group learned about sustainable development so they could give presentations in schools, and we planned to show the Mongolians how to do things like facilitating meetings, lobbying, doing school presentations, and running campaigns. But they saw it as us just coming to do presentations to schools on sustainable development, while we were trying to get the message across that we wanted to help them learn how to do that *themselves*. So it was quite trying but very interesting.

I loved observing how our group related to what was happening. When you're not in work or education you get labelled and that's a horrible thing but a couple of the young people really developed and their minds opened in new ways. I was fascinated by one particular guy who transcended his situation. When there were Mongolians who didn't speak English, he would sit next to them and somehow find a way to have a conversation and make a connection. It was incredible.

What did you do after you left university?

The year after I graduated, the UN Climate Change Negotiations were due to be held in Qatar. There was some frustration because there had never been any Arab youth voices in the negotiations but Qatar was felt to be a good place to start as it's the home country of Al-Jazeera and so was more likely to get attention. I volunteered to work with an organisation called IndyAct which is based in Lebanon and I lived in Beirut for two months. While I was there I helped to establish the Arab Youth Climate Movement and dealt with the logistics of getting over fifty young people from the region, to Qatar—things like getting UN accreditation, visas from all over the Arab world, printing T-shirts and banners, organising hotels, and so on.

Lebanon is a tiny country and they think they're the best at everything and *want* the best of everything—fast cars, expensive bars, designer clothes, and there's lots of peer pressure to drink. It's all very glossy and I felt very plain. But I had a quirky landlady and the food was amazing. The language was fine too because everyone speaks English or French.

I think I was very naïve when I arrived. Fourteen foreigners had recently been kidnapped and I was all by myself. I didn't even have anyone picking me up at the airport. It was basically OK but there *were* some uncomfortable moments particularly when a car bomb went off very close to my house and killed one of the ministers. That was very scary and no-one knew why it had happened. There was speculation that Syria was behind it with Assad trying to stir up tension in Lebanon. My parents said I must come home but there were burning tyres around the airport and there was no way I could have flown. I stayed in the house for a couple of days until things calmed down, and then carried on in Lebanon until it was time to go to the UN Climate Negotiations in Qatar.

After that I went to Egypt. That came about because I'd met an Egyptian delegate at the UNESCO forum the year before. He was my age and told me what it was like to be involved in the Arab Spring uprisings. I hadn't known anything about what was going on in Egypt and we talked for a couple of hours. His whole face lit up and his stories were incredible. He talked about things that most people in this country will never experience, like being shot at. He challenged me on so many levels—history, politics, all kinds of things. So I went to Egypt to follow up on that and to try and set up a Zero Carbon Egypt project. I took a lot of ideas from the Centre for Alternative Technology in Wales.

I love Cairo. It's like a Middle Eastern London in the middle of the desert. Everything is grand—it's beautiful and fascinating, and the people are so nice.

What's the Zero Carbon Egypt project?

After the uprising, Egypt needed development proposals, and I was interested in researching the impact of all the different energy sources—how they affect the environment, communities, jobs, and all sorts of other things. We know, for example, that coal causes widespread lung disease, as well as water pollution and water scarcity. All of this research had been done elsewhere but not in the Arab world. So that's what I did for a year and a half—I coordinated the Environmental Justice Programme which focuses on energy, coal and water pollution. It covers both environmental concerns and social justice. Those two things are not often put together.

The UK's rivers are polluted but in comparison to many other places they really are quite clean. It takes a lot of regulation and enforcement to keep them in this state and the problem in Egypt is that it has regulation but it doesn't have enforcement. The major polluters are industries with deep connections to the Government so a blind eye is turned to what they do. The main population centres are along the Nile and the poorer you are, the more reliant you are on the Nile water for drinking, fishing, washing, cleaning, and agriculture. And that stuff is filthy—it's full of pollutants from tanning, the chemical industry and food processing. Agriculture, too. They use so much pesticide. They douse the crops because there are no instructions and the pests die so they assume that pesticides are a good thing. It's a huge problem and there's no monitoring so no-one knows the extent of it. We started a map with citizen reporting as a way of gauging problems that need more investigation. It was also a way of engaging with people on a local level so they take ownership of what they do. We challenged the Government and if we hadn't pushed so hard there wouldn't be any regulations for coal usage, and now there are.

You've done so much, Megan. What are you proudest of?

That's a good question. I'm proud of the fact that I went to a Middle Eastern country. Most environmentalists won't touch the Middle East with a bargepole because of the oil production. And Egypt is massive. Also that I managed to engage average Egyptians who thought I was crazy for caring about this kind of stuff. They all thought I was just a stupid foreigner and an idealist. Now a couple of years later, many of them see that decarbonised development just has to be the way to go, and even the World Bank is funding this. It was also good to go to a country where there's little capacity but lots of enthusiasm. To be able to say, "This is what's being done in other places in the world and this is how to make sure you're progressive and don't fall into the same potholes as other countries." And I've tried to find young women to replace me, sometimes in ways that they may not have considered. When I left Egypt I got my best friend there to take over as head of the Environmental Justice Programme. She's younger than me and was convinced that she couldn't do it. I said she could.

What are the main things that people can do to have less impact on the environment?

I don't think that people understand how much impact flying has. Basically it's one of the worst things you can do. If you're a vegan and you cycle everywhere for a year and then you take one flight you'll have negated all the good that you've done. Flying is one of the major cultural things that we have to tackle in developed countries. People do it without thinking when there are other options like going to Europe by bus or train. Even driving a car is better than flying.

Food waste is another important topic. And I believe in buying food that's local and organic but not at terrible inflated prices. I want us to get to a place where it's just a given that those things are readily available. I also believe that it's not just about cutting back but instead putting your money into the right things. So, for example, going with a renewable energy provider or spending money on public transport. Lots of those things are positive and exciting.

Who are your heroes?

No-one high profile but my personal heroes are the strong women who brought me up—my mum, my grandmother, my aunt, and my godmother. My grandmother lived next door and was a designer. She was very cultured and never did anything conventionally. She refused to wear beige, had perfect taste and always looked fantastic. In lots of ways, she was very selfish and dominant but also fascinating. Then there was my aunt, my mum's younger sister, who was warm and wonderful and gave massive hugs. My mum is fastidious, sensitive, kind, and always on time. She ran the family restaurant business for years and is very strong. My godmother has been a nurse for much of her life. She's very open and interested in everybody. Each of those women in their different ways, has been essential to me.

November 2015

Mala

"The detention centres were horrible. Absolutely horrible."

A few months have passed and now that I have the first two links in place I'm feeling more confident about the project. When I started with Kirsti we had my cousin as a mutual point of reference but as I progress along the chain it's important that each interviewee has a positive experience so that they're willing to introduce me to whichever friend or colleague they choose for the next link.

Megan has passed me on to Mala. They first met at university but are now housemates. So once again I'm on an early evening train to London and am heading for a wine bar. There aren't any other suitable options at this time of day in this area, and this one is near the City law firm where Mala works. It's a dark February evening and the rain is torrential. I always forget to carry an umbrella but Mala is friendly and politely ignores my bedraggled appearance.

It quickly becomes clear that there are many potential topics we could cover. Mala is a founder member of an online feminist group called Wolf Whistled and is particularly interested in transgender politics, and the effect that internet pornography has on young mens' attitudes to women. These are certainly things she cares about but this evening we focus on her day job—human rights law.

What's really important to you, Mala?

At the moment I'm working as a paralegal in the immigration department of a big law firm. It's quite a complicated area, but human rights law is what I was most passionate about when I left university.

How did you get interested in human rights?

All kinds of societies grab your interest at university and when I went to Bristol I got involved with Student Action for Refugees. During my second year I went to a weekend conference in London and they got people who'd been granted refugee status in the UK to speak about their experiences. One of them was a Burmese man—there was something about the space and the number of people there that made it incredibly emotive—it sounds a bit of a cliché but it was a turning point for me. He was clearly a very intelligent man and was doing well in his studies in Burma. But he was also in a student organisation that was attempting to revolt against the Government and he was punished for that by being held in a pit of maggots. At one point they submerged his head. It was the way he told it—I just thought, "How on earth can these things actually happen to people?" It's really easy to be totally disconnected. There's so much disbelief around and I don't believe half the stories I hear but to be in a room with someone who's been through this, and is looking at you—there was absolutely no way I could have sat there and said I didn't believe him. It was also extraordinary to see that he had survived and built a completely new life. He was working for the BBC.

So there was that, but my interest also came from going

into Bristol and getting to know other organisations, like City of Sanctuary which raises awareness of the needs of refugees and asylum seekers and helps local organisations to deliver services to them. Within the space of six months I went from knowing very little about asylum seekers and refugee rights to it being something that consumed all my time and energy. My parents thought it was a bit of a fad and that I'd go on to find other more interesting things.

What else did you do to get involved?

As part of my French and German degree I spent a year abroad and six months of that was in Berlin. Attitudes throughout Western Europe tend to be quite similar with regard to asylum seekers and refugees—*Well, it's a bit crap but it's not our problem.* But I lived in quite a hippy household and we got involved with blockading a road. It was because the police were trying to evict a group of asylum seekers from the house where they were squatting.

Then when I got back to university for the fourth year my friend Liv and I decided to run Student Action for Refugees, in Bristol. It was a big commitment and I was struggling in my grammar modules. I needed to put a lot of time into trying to pull those marks up to make sure I got a 2:1 but much of the time when I was in the library I'd be on my laptop typing up notes from meetings or on the phone trying to find spaces for events. One thing we did was to organise a sleep-out to highlight that there are lots of destitute asylum seekers in the UK. They're given something like £35 a week to live on. That has to cover everything including their food and travel expenses. Students from the society joined in this big sleep-out and we had a lot of homeless people with us, too. It was a really cold night—quite extraordinarily freezing in fact. I don't know how much it achieved but it was definitely a wake-up call for me. It raised awareness with lots of people who had no idea about these things and our local MP came down to support it.

By the end of my fourth year I'd spoken to a lot of people and realised something important about myself. Some people are good at campaigning—they lobby and try to create change. The trouble was that the problems seemed so big and I wasn't sure where to start or whether I'd achieve anything so I didn't feel well suited to that. But the thing you hear again and again within the refugee community is that there's a need for good lawyers. So I decided to move back home to London and do a law conversion course. After that I did my Legal Practice Course. It took two years to get through all of that, and then I started at a Legal Aid firm doing asylum human rights work for people in detention. That involved visiting detention centres at Dover and the ones near Heathrow and Gatwick.

What are the detention centres like?

My best friend is a theatre director and when I started this work she'd just directed a play called *Eye of a Needle* which was about a detention centre. It showed random waiting rooms where Home Office staff and legal aid representatives just sat and talked to one another. It got incredible reviews but even so it seemed rather unbelievable. Then the first time that I turned up at a detention centre, Harmondsworth near Heathrow, it was exactly like that. I've never seen so many locked doors. I've spoken to people who've worked in prisons and I think there are more locked doors in detention centres than there are in most prisons.

You walk in and go through the first building where you have to log in and get a badge. There's a waiting room and once you become well versed in what's going on then you know to go through to the back. Then you end up at another check-in desk where they log you in again and you go through a door. When that closes you're in quite a small space like being vacuum-packed. Next, another door opens and someone does a full body search on you. They tell you to open your mouth and take off your shoes. And then you're led through to another waiting area. You wait there for a while and then the guard takes you through to a third building where it smells really clinical, and you see your client in an upstairs room. The rooms where the detainees live are next to this and although you never get to see those rooms, the walls are very thin. When I was at Colnbrook someone had committed suicide and the detainees were trying to get a proper investigation. I could hear very loud protests.

The first time I went to Harmondsworth it had just been taken over by Mitie, a big security company. Before that, it was run by G4S. It was horrible. Absolutely horrible. I cried.

What was it that made you cry?

It was meeting my first client. He was an incredibly sweet man from Kerala in Southern India, and reminded me of one of my Dad's cousins. He was very educated and spoke fantastic English. Anyway, he'd been in the UK illegally for about ten years and had made a life for himself. He was trying to make a human rights claim so he could stay here but it was a hopeless case. I had to ask if he wanted to make an asylum claim because that's what was on the questionnaire. And he said, "Why do people keep asking me this? I don't feel any persecution where I've come from. Are you asking me to lie? I've been here for ten years and I've lots of things to offer. I want to do anything I can to stay here but I'm not a liar—I've got my dignity." There was something very humble about him. He was a single man in his fifties who didn't know anyone in the centre and he was wearing a pair of flip flops in the middle of winter. What touched me was the clarity with which he said that although he wanted to stay he wasn't going to lie about it. A lot of people are willing to lie in order to get what they want—I don't know that I wouldn't do that if the boot was on the other foot. In so many situations I'd think that if only the law was written in another way there would be people who'd be able to remain here. But it was my job to apply the law, not to question it and however much agility I might have had, there was no way that his situation would allow him to stay.

I had to do a basic exam to do that job but it didn't prepare me at all for being faced with people who have really terrible problems. You go in saying, "I'm here as your legal representative." But all you're actually saying is, "I'm here as another human being who has supposedly done enough training to help you."

What other impressions did you get of detention centres?

There are nine detention centres in the UK, and Harmondsworth is the biggest. It's got about 600 detainees. But people also get held in prison under immigration detention laws. So overall, there are thousands and thousands of people locked up.

In the detention centres it's not like the detainees have nothing—I've heard people say that they'd rather be in there than on the street as it's warm. They aren't malnourished but they *are* denied absolutely all of their freedom. There's really high barbed wire, and yellow light all the time. And they have no idea when they're going to get out. At least with criminal issues you know the maximum sentence you have to serve but in a detention centre there's no onus on anyone to say when you'll get out. Some people have been in detention for seven or eight years.

Another really horrible thing is that if you're detained for more than four weeks you have a 90% chance of developing a mental health problem. At first I was overwhelmed but then quite quickly I became hardened to it. I worked with a couple of great people who really were in it to help the detainees. I also worked with a lot of people who just did it as a nine-to-five job and knew that by ticking the boxes then Legal Aid would pay them even if at the end of the year they'd won very few cases. To be honest I don't blame them for that because the whole system is so confused.

There were some fast-track cases going on when I was there. Those are claims which the Home Office deals with in a matter of two weeks by doing back-to-back interviews.

What triggers a fast-track case?

It's something that's just got bigger and bigger over the past ten years. There's a question over whether the fast-track system is lawful because it doesn't give claimants enough time to collate their evidence. But the Home Office's response is that there are so many unfounded asylum claims being made that we shouldn't give people the chance to wait in the country for months on end.

I'm clearly naïve. I thought you were saying it was recognised that some people are in very difficult circumstances so they're being helped quicker.

I wish that was the reason. That would be lovely.

The UK Government often disbelieves single men who come to the UK via Calais. The fact is that most of the refugees in the camp in Calais are men and they need to be fairly healthy and strong to get away from wherever they were. Travelling overland to Calais with small children is incredibly difficult and so people are very unlikely to bring young children with them from a war torn country or from where they're being persecuted.

At the moment if you're a refugee with children and you *are* able to get to Calais and bring them over the border into the UK this is one of the only things that's given more weight. If you arrive with children then the likelihood is they're not going to send you away—at least not until those children reach seventeen and are re-evaluated as adults.

So that's some of what I saw in the detention centres and it's something I would really love to go back to when I have more experience. At the moment I'm in a law firm with a mixture of practices. I'm in the immigration team and do solely private work. The firm doesn't do any Legal Aid work.

What's private immigration work?

It's very different from detention work. I do a lot of naturalisations. That's when someone has been in the country for the necessary amount of time and they're ready to apply to become a British citizen. That's a straightforward application. I also do a lot of spouse applications. That's when a British citizen has met someone abroad and wants to bring them to the UK. The regulations have become more restrictive recently. Now British citizens have to show that they're earning at least £18,600 in the UK in order to bring their partner here, and if there are children then it's more on top of that. I'm also doing a lot of EU work at the moment, especially around Brexit. There are panic applications coming in—people who've been resident in the UK for years and years completely legally, but are worrying that they're going to be kicked out if we leave the EU.

Then there are the Tier 1 applications. I feel uncomfortable with those. If you have £2,000,000 that you can invest in UK bonds then you get a free pass to live in the UK. You can work, study or just live off your money. It's funny because they're often quite lovely people that you wouldn't know are sitting on lots of cash and investing it for visa purposes. What I find really tricky is when I know that people are moving their money to the UK because they'll end up paying less tax here than in their own country. But I'm learning a lot and it's the kind of training that will make me into a good solicitor if I eventually get a training contract here. I'm working with absolutely brilliant people.

And you've been to the refugee camp in Calais?

I've been three times now. The first time, my boyfriend and I were part of a group of about a hundred people who cycled on donated bikes from London to Dover and got the ferry across. The camp's about a mile away and when you get there it's suddenly not about you and your bike and the hundred people, it's about the three thousand people in the camp. We left the bikes there because when the refugees go to be interviewed by the French authorities about their immigration claims, they have to walk six miles or so. It was August when we went, and quite a nice day and some people made coffee for us in their makeshift house. The second time, I went with my friend Liv from university, and we took a big carload of donations. Everyone there is desperate for shoes. It was October and it was starting to get cold. When we opened up the car full of donations it felt like being swarmed. It was an absolute frenzy with people wanting to see what was in it.

The camp is just completely open land with lots and lots of tents on it where people live in pretty horrible conditions. It went from three thousand to six thousand people in the space of a few months and it's had a lot of media attention. Now the authorities have started demolishing bits of the camp with bulldozers. It's a bit like a weird game. There are people there on the ground who pick up on what's happening. They tell volunteers from the UK and other places who rush over in an attempt to help. They move all the tents and the next thing you know, the whole thing has been demolished. Then the refugees have to start building things again.

There were two iconic buildings in the camp—the great church and a big mosque. And just recently the authorities demolished both of those as well. They're saying that they need to clear the land and eventually move the camp because it's too close to the residential areas. Some of the interviews with these residents are quite extraordinary. Having said that, I can't imagine there are many people who would want a huge refugee camp to be next to their house. I can see where their frustration comes from. But not their hostility and anger—some of that is absolutely appalling.

Can you sum up what you feel about the work you've done so far?

I've come across asylum seekers who are fleeing persecution and also people who have no human rights claims at all and just want to live in the UK. But basically when it comes down to it, we're all human. And it makes me realise that those of us who live here are just so lucky.

February 2016

Holly

"I like to direct plays that feel cleverer than me"

In our conversation Mala mentioned a friend who is a theatre director, and now I'm going to meet her as she is the next link in the chain. Mala has told me that Holly is particularly interested in feminism and climate change. She adds that she's a very interesting woman and is currently working at the National Theatre.

Once again, I'm on a train to London. It's a Spring afternoon and I'm heading for the South Bank where I've arranged to meet Holly at the Royal Festival Hall café.

I wasn't sure when I started the project whether people would be willing to open up about their lives. So it's reassuring when I meet Holly that she, like the previous links is friendly and that there's no hint of reticence or suspicion. "It's ***such*** *an interesting project," she says warmly. She has lots to say and talks fast which is always an asset in an interviewee as we get to cover more ground. She tells me about things that have proved difficult in her career so far. Her honesty is impressive and I can appreciate that introspection is a valuable tool in her directing. She's had to learn how to collaborate better and how to deal with bad publicity. And she is* ***very*** *clear that drawing room comedies are not for her—she wants to direct the kind of theatre that is intellectually and conceptually challenging, the sort that you can only work on if you believe it has integrity and truth.*

What are you doing at the moment, Holly?

I'm associate director on *People, Places and Things* which started at the National Theatre, and is now in the West End. Once a show is up and running then the director goes off and directs other things but you still need to sustain the quality of that show whilst it's on. So, as associate director, that's what I do. It involves various things like rehearsing understudies and also watching the show once or twice a week. I take a load of notes and then disseminate them amongst the actors. It's important to keep everything alive and fresh because shows get stale very quickly when they're on eight times a week.

It's a strong play about addiction and also about therapy. We realised quite quickly in the rehearsal room that almost everyone has a story about addiction whether it's their own story or their mother's story, or a friend of a friend. We could have made a version of this play that used those experiences and which presented some kind of truthfulness on stage. But this subject is a matter of life and death for people and we're in a context where it's being served up for entertainment. So it felt really important to ground it in research. We worked with two rehabilitation centres—one's a tiny place in Catford which is massively underfunded and the other is The Priory which is a private clinic.

People who've been through the Alcoholics Anonymous (AA) programme are so practised at opening up and sharing—you get a huge amount of generosity in those environments and the willingness of people to wear their heart on their sleeve is dumbfounding. It makes you realise how private most of us are and how going through the AA steps gives you an opportunity to really get to know yourself.

Perhaps everyone would benefit from this. Before the play opened we invited groups from both centres to watch a rehearsal room run. That's when it's just the play—no lighting, costumes or special effects and to watch it with those people was staggeringly moving. Denise Gough is the lead actor and the way she rages against her rescuers is so accurate and truthful that you can't quite believe it's fiction.

Is the play about drug addiction or alcoholism?

Ah that's interesting. It's about both. The generation above me tends to distinguish the two, but my generation just seems to talk about addiction. That's because if you get through being an alcoholic, say, then often you're susceptible to other things and you shift to some other kind of addiction like sex, porn or just loads of late night television.

Another thing I discovered is that addiction is not discriminatory. If you sat in a room with The Priory and Catford clients all mixed together you would struggle to divide them into their groups. I'd guessed in a middle-class, naïve, prejudiced way that addiction is something that affects people when they hit rock bottom. But I learned that it is indiscriminate. Just because you're homeless doesn't mean you're going to become an addict. It takes a specific kind of wiring in your brain to be susceptible to that.

How did you get into theatre directing?

I guess it started with my dad. He's always been interested in theatre and as a child I got taken to some really whacky fringe things. So for me, theatre was a bit like reading—it was something I knew how to do. I joined a drama group when I was at primary school and discovered quickly that I possessed a muscle that was about seeing the big picture and knowing how to improve things. By the time I got to secondary school I started to realise that this might be directing, and when I got to university I thought, "That IS directing." I ran the drama society there and by the time I left, I was very clear that I wanted to be a director.

Then someone told me about the directing course at Birkbeck, so I applied on a whim and got a place. There were various group emails over that summer and I had an inkling that I might be the only woman on the course and sure enough when I arrived in September, it was me and nine men. I think that was just a quirk as another year they had nine women and one man. But it *is* the case that the theatre industry is dominated by white Oxbridge-educated men and a lot of my class *were* white men who had just graduated from Oxford or Cambridge. I think that men often have a sense of entitlement about getting into directing and that makes it easier for them.

Anyway, I had an extraordinary two years. I'd studied English at university which was very female-heavy and on this course I spent a lot of time with men. And I'm so grateful for that experience. Firstly, because I've now got a whole load of clever, brilliant friends but also because I had to examine my social behaviour in such a microscopic way that it propelled me into feminism.

One of the key moments was sitting in the pub with those nine boys having a very heated discussion about pornography. And realising that all of the men in my life, except probably my dad, have consumed pornography regularly and I was just clueless about it. Genuinely clueless. I thought that pornography was something that a few people did from time to time. I just didn't realise that it was a daily part of the lives of people that I love. I spent over a week feeling betrayed by the other sex and out of that anger came a need to talk about gender. This year I've directed two plays specifically about porn.

How was the course at Birkbeck?

The attitude on the course is 'We can't teach you how to direct but we can teach you how to collaborate with all the people you need to work with.' It was a crash course in learning what all the other artists do—like set designers, lighting designers, sound designers, and movement directors. The first year is seminar-based and the second year you have an industry placement. I went to the Royal Exchange Theatre in Manchester.

It was the first time I'd been an assistant director and it was really hard for my ego. I've always had problems with hierarchy and authority and that really flared up there. It's taken me four years to learn what assistant directing is, to appreciate it and to see this as a time to hone my craft.

What impact did that placement have on you?

It made me let go of the reins, and I learned how to collaborate better. When I was at university, it was always about me and my vision. I knew the right way and I couldn't listen to other peoples' ideas whereas I now know that you're stronger when you take the best idea in the room. That best idea might come from your stage manager or an actor or anyone else whose thoughts are bubbling away. I found the placement emotional but I was extremely lucky as I worked with a lot of wonderful women who have since looked out for me. I didn't realise how badly I needed a female role model until I was given one. Like we all do, I left university thinking that I could change the world and do whatever I wanted. I naively thought, "I'll write to the Royal Court and tell them I'm a director." But going into the workforce taught me that people don't see youth that way, and I learned about the industry as much as about the job. I think I'm now very savvy about the politics and the networking.

What are you most proud of so far?

I worked with the final year students at Royal Central School of Speech and Drama and directed *The Low Road* by Bruce Norris. It's a contemporary play and really deep. With every single sentence you can unpack imagery and metaphor. I worked with twenty keen young actors and as a group they were very political. I wanted to bring my own political ideas into my working life and we did some bold things. It was an exciting time. We set up a mini occupy camp in the garden area outside the theatre, with no explanation. So when people arrived it looked like there was a student occupation going on. And during the performance a group of protesters took over the conference that was in the play. It was really interesting that some people at Central worried about us setting up this protest without a piece of cardboard that said, 'This is not a student occupation; this is a piece of art.' They were very rigid about it and put real constraints on what we were allowed to do. And we felt like it was important not to do it like that.

I also had lots of personal discoveries during that time. I've always thought I was good at the psychological side of directing—carefully micromanaging the relationships between the characters on stage and analysing their conflicts and desires. But directing *The Low Road* with so many actors made me realise that I have a hunger and the skill set, to make broader brushstrokes—to create images and atmospheres. It's about zooming out and realising that I have to trust my actors to make the micro-psychological decisions. My job is to look after the bigger picture—the dramaturgical side of the storytelling.

What's been the most difficult challenge?

That's a good question. I recently worked with a writer and we got the idea for a show from a *Daily Mail* story. It was about a young woman who went to Magaluf and gave twenty-one blow jobs to men on the dance floor in exchange for an exotic holiday that she thought she was going to win. But *exotic holiday* turned out to be the name of a cocktail. The media went crazy—there's a video of her doing it that went viral and she got absolutely slut-shamed. Yet there's never been any coverage of the men who participated. No-one knows who they are, and why aren't *they* being slut-shamed? So Milly the writer and I made a play about a young woman called Nicola who goes to Ibiza and does something very similar. When she gets back home, the press is camped outside her house. But the twist we wanted to explore was what would happen if at every point the central protagonist, Nicola, doesn't do what society expects a female to do. So she never breaks down, she never says that she's disgusted with herself and she very confidently sets up a porn booth business in London—like photo booths but where you can go in and make a high-quality home porn movie.

Anyway, we made this show above a pub in South London and in the build up to the show, the press coverage went insane. At one point we were the fifth most clicked-on link on the BBC website. The tickets sold very well and people wanted to do interviews with us. Then over a period of about two weeks we got some terrible reviews and simultaneously the show sold out. It was horrendous to be told by some of the press that this was bad but to know that two thousand people were coming to see it. There's something ironic about experiencing public shaming whilst making a piece of work which is about public shaming. I have to admit that some of the reviews were spot on—there *were* dramaturgical problems that we hadn't addressed. And I learned a brilliant lesson which is not to get into bed with scripts that aren't ready. But I felt that the reviews tended to be very sexist. If I'd been a man and made that show, I might not have got any more stars, but I'm sure I wouldn't have got the same write-up.

I'm through the emotion of it now but it really damaged my self-confidence as a director. It was a rite of passage and was going to happen at some point but it was very early on in my career. A friend who is a brilliant director said, "Welcome to the real world, Holly. My review carnage was on the Olivier stage at the National. It happens."

I survived it. I'd survive it again. I have to—that's the nature of the game.

What are the best and worst things about your work?

At its best, it's about being in a room with amazing, creative people and thinking, "I'm getting paid to do this. We're making art and people are going to turn up and engage with it." And I think that the theatre industry is starting to shake itself up and that's really exciting. There are a few amazing women in positions of power such as Vicky Featherstone at the Royal Court and Erica Whyman at the RSC. At its worst, it's a freelance, unstructured lifestyle with odd hours and like all freelance artists I live in fear that I'll never work again. Though I am planning to take this summer off and try to be guilt-free about it.

What do you want to do next?

At parties people will say, "Oh my God, you're a theatre director. That's incredible." So it's easy to think that you're quirky and that you're doing something alternative, but actually within the theatre industry I've followed a very mainstream route. I haven't consciously done that but I have had a sheep experience—this is how you succeed at school, this is how you succeed at university, this is how you succeed in a career. Then recently I thought that if I just carry on ticking boxes in my career then my twenties are going to evaporate so I need to be brave and step off the treadmill. I'd like to direct plays that change society—texts that I feel are cleverer than me and push me intellectually and conceptually.

There's a wave of German-influenced theatre in London at the moment. German theatre is very distinctive and bold and outrageous—animalistic, sexualised, transgender, non-binary. In English theatre we might read a play and think, "Oh it takes place in a living room so that's what the set will be," whereas in Berlin, they might read it and say, "This feels like it's to do with freedom. Let's set it in cages and wear things on our faces that stop us speaking." They come at things from outside the box.

At the moment I work in prison twice a year and I'd like to continue doing that. It's emotionally expensive but it's very fulfilling to be working there with a professional set of skills. When you're at the top of the theatre industry you make brilliant, polished work for middle class audiences that are very used to enjoying that kind of thing. And that's as far as the show goes. Whereas working on plays with pockets of society that aren't your average white, middle class theatregoer then you really see the power of theatre. When it's in its own little bubble being self-referential, and fulfilling a certain demographic's expectation of what it should be then it's easy to lose sight of that power.

When you work in prison you see people learning lines and performing and being part of making something. And it recharges their self-confidence in a way that it doesn't for your average actor. I was in Brixton the other day having coffee with a friend and I heard, "Holly, Holly." It was one of the boys that I'd just finished a project with and he's now out of jail and working in music production.

Would you take on the direction of a Noel Coward play, for example? Something that's very established and middle class.

No, I think I'd find it boring.

April 2016

Susan W

"You want the recognition...then you have it and it's scary"

Holly's handover was characteristically warm: "Susie is an actress and I've worked with her three times—twice at the Royal Exchange Theatre in Manchester and once at the National Theatre. She never ceases to inspire me both as a person and in her craft. You'll love her!"

It transpires during my later email exchanges with Susan as she signs herself, that although she lives in London, she is currently filming a TV series in Bristol. She's happy to meet me but never knows for sure what her schedule will be until the day before. We tentatively agree to meet one afternoon as most of the filming is being done at night and so I set off for Bristol by train and take the short walk from Temple Meads Station to the flat above a branch of Sainsbury's, which is her home for the next few weeks.

One of the things I'm already loving about these interviews is getting an insider's view into other worlds. I go to the theatre whenever I can but by talking with Holly I realise that I've never thought much about the director's role, but I am sure I will on future theatre visits. One thing she mentioned is that a director has to trust the actors as it's their job to analyse the characters' conflicts and desires and to bring this to their acting. Susan takes this one step further, describing ***how*** *she gets inside the psyche of a character. She also gives wise advice on how to deal with that most difficult of challenges—professional rejection.*

How did you get into acting, Susan?

Well, I suppose it all dates back to when I was about ten and first went to the theatre. It was for a friend's birthday and we went to see *Bugsy Malone* in the West End. There were children in it and I now know from researching what I saw, that it was a National Youth Theatre show, but I didn't know anything about that at the time. I remember leaving and feeling really weird. For days after, my Mum kept asking me how I was because I was so quiet. I didn't understand why, but now I know it was because I was thinking, "God, I want to do that," and being sad that I wasn't able to. I sort of ignored the feeling and then when I was at secondary school I had an English teacher who gave me a leaflet about the National Youth Theatre and suggested I apply. It was only ten pounds in those days, so I saved up my pocket money and got in. I still didn't really understand what it was and we didn't have the internet at home so I couldn't research it. Some time later I realised that all these famous actors like Helen Mirren and Tom Courtenay had come through it.

What do you think your English teacher spotted in you?

I have no idea because we didn't do any drama at school. My first taste of it was with the National Youth Theatre on a two-week summer course, and that's when I got bitten by it. After that I wanted to do more so I joined a Saturday drama group. It was run by English National Opera and it was about ten pounds a term—stuff that doesn't exist these days. We did an hour of singing, an hour of dance and an hour of drama. My singing teacher was Gareth Malone. It was before he got into the Royal Academy of Music and he was very young. I found singing really traumatic but he was very big on everyone finding their voice. He pushed me and was really inspiring. It was him and my drama teacher who were the first to tell me I should apply for drama school. I didn't even really know what it was, so they explained. I remember Gareth saying, "You should go to RADA—of course you should go to RADA—why not?" and being really stern with me. And I did go to RADA.

What did drama school do for you?

I got my first agent when I was about seventeen and then I worked on a TV drama. It was a show called *That Summer Day* about the London bombings. It was from the perspective of six children and I was one of them. It was great to be in it but I was working on gut instinct—some takes felt really good and others were just dreadful. At that stage I didn't really know why and drama school helped with that.

Drama school also taught me to trust my instinct and skills. That means that I don't have to hassle the director and ask, "How was that? Was I good?" It made me self-sufficient. That's especially important in TV. You don't really have rehearsals and the director doesn't have much time to give you, so you need to turn up on Day One, ready to go. Drama school's a good preparation because you work on so many texts and with so many different people. And they teach you all these skills that at the time you think you're never going to use. But they're like a tool box and you suddenly find you're in a job where you need them. So for instance, we did animal work at drama school. We had to be pandas and other animals and I enjoyed it but I thought, "I'm never going to use that!" And then I played a character in a National Theatre play called *Hotel*. She was pretending to be a maid but actually she was planning to hold a family hostage. I didn't know how to become physically robust when I was dressed in a little maid's outfit. Then I thought, "I'll try something with animals." I picked a panther because the character was very slow and measured at the beginning of the play but then she pounced. I didn't tell my director or anyone else what I was doing—it was just in my head. If I hadn't gone to drama school then I wouldn't have known anything like that.

Another challenge is when you have to act and aren't feeling great. Often things happen before you go on set—a friend of mine saw someone jump in front of a train. And when I was making the film *Half of a Yellow Sun* in Nigeria, my dad passed away. The next day I had to be on set and it was really horrible but I was able to put my feelings on one side. I just had to think in a technical way, "What is it that I'm trying to do to this person? Am I trying to humiliate them?" You pick a word and it just sees you through. I couldn't bring myself to watch the film for ages. But when I did, I don't think you'd have been able tell that anything had been going on. That was the moment when I thought, "That's why I went to drama school—so I can do my job even when I'm under stress."

Where do you find your confidence?

A lot of becoming an actor was to do with other people spotting something in me and being encouraging. But there came a point after I left drama school when I had to get my confidence from myself. And what took over was my enjoyment—I really love acting. I enjoy the stories and the opportunity to play different people. As an actor you're not in a position to pick and choose parts, certainly when you're starting out. But I think I've been really lucky to play a variety of characters and I've done a lot of theatre that's had a social conscience to it.

So for me, the goal was finding something I enjoy. My parents came over from Nigeria to make a better life for my sister and me, and I saw how hard things were for them. My mum worked nights and my dad always did two or three jobs and really suffered. My confidence comes from feeling lucky that I've found something that I love, and I don't think that happens for everyone.

What's difficult about being an actor?

The thing about acting and other arts jobs is that talent isn't tangible—it's so objective. For every hundred people that think you're great, there'll be five who think you're not very good. And you can win awards and there'll still be people that say, "Actually I don't think you're very good." So it's hard to get to a point where you can feel, "I'm really good at this." If you want to be a lawyer then you pass the Bar exams and you can say, "I'm a lawyer." That's it—you're a lawyer. But being an actor is different. There's nothing that makes you feel that you're in the right place. Even when you're on really big jobs there's that feeling that you're a fraud. I remember Kate Winslet doing an interview where she read an extract from her diary that said, "I feel horrible—everyone hates me—I can't act." And she'd been acting since she was a child.

Also actors are really vulnerable because there's so much rejection. Being turned down for parts is something that you have to make friends with but it's very difficult to do. One of my friends auditioned recently and got really close to getting the part she wanted. When she didn't get it, she said, "Next time I'm not going to put so much effort in." And I said, "Next time you should put all the effort in and you still might not get it. But you need to make friends with that heartbreak." Some people are fragile and find the rejection very hard. There are all kinds of reasons why you don't get parts. It doesn't mean you can't act, but it might be that you're too short, too big, too small, you've got dark hair, you're not famous enough... That sort of thing can drive you mad but you just have to say, "OK that's fine."

The visibility is an issue, too. I realised a while ago, that if someone wanted to know about me then it's easy to find out that I'll be on stage at a particular theatre at 7.30. When I had that thought it made me feel really weird. And another is that when things don't go well then the actors are the most vulnerable. No-one's going to say, "That film flopped because of the second assistant director—I'll never work with them again." They'll be employed regardless. But when things go wrong then people are critical of us first. I get people saying things like, "You look so ugly on TV," especially since I worked on *Chewing Gum*. People feel they can say anything and behave in certain ways to you. And I'm not famous so I can't imagine what it's like if you are. Psychologically you want the recognition and then you have it, and it's scary.

You just mentioned *Chewing Gum*—that's been very big hasn't it?

Yes, we're doing a second series. Michaela Coel the writer and actor, won a couple of BAFTAs for it. I got involved because I'd done a play with Michaela and she invited me to audition. It's always flattering when friends ask you to be in things but I take it with a pinch of salt. And then I got the part after one audition. That almost never happens especially when it's a regular part in a series. At the time I'd accepted a part in a play with Maxine Peake at the Royal Exchange in Manchester. It looked like it was going to work out but then the filming for *Chewing Gum* got moved back twice and the start date for both projects was the same day. So I had to make a very difficult decision. I chose the TV show but I felt like I was letting people down. Then I got an email from Maxine Peake. She said, "I would be really upset if you'd taken this play instead of the TV show. We need more women like you on TV so hopefully we'll get to play together at some other time." Most of us have been in this situation and she really understood.

When we got to the first day of filming I was so nervous and I thought, "It had better be really good after all this hassle." And it was great. I did about two weeks on it. Michaela and the crew really trusted me with the character so I could do a lot of what I wanted. It's gone down really well.

I had a tiny role in the *Inbetweeners 2* movie and having that on my CV, opened doors. It's been the same with *Chewing Gum.*

What are you doing at the moment?

I'm working on an E4/Netflix series called *Crazyhead* and it's written by Howard Overman who created *Misfits, Atlantis* and *Merlin.* I play Raquel, one of the leads and it's about two self-made demon hunters. It's billed as a comedy horror series. It's the biggest thing that I've ever done on screen so it's a lot of responsibility and a lot of words. I'm really enjoying it.

What else are you doing?

I'm developing my own TV series as a writer and performer. It was inspired by my time filming in Nigeria. I'd never met my family there before, but during a gap in the schedule I went off to Port Harcourt and met my grandparents, cousins, aunts, uncles and my half-sister for the first time. It was really overwhelming but also incredibly funny and moving. I suddenly found I'd got all this family and so my TV series is about a Nigerian-British character who discovers a sister in Nigeria and brings her back to England. It's about identity and where you're from.

Your family must be very proud of you...

I realised early on that it was very important to me that my family were proud of me. But to be honest I think my parents weren't overjoyed when I became an actor. Whenever they didn't turn up to see plays, it really hurt. So I learned quite quickly that it's my job and there's no point doing it to show off to people or to impress them. Now I just get on with it. I think, though, that my mum's very impressed that I said I would do it and now I can live off it. That was her worry—that I'd be as poor as they were.

Is there a piece of work that you are proudest of?

The part I played in *Hotel* was very physical. And I'm proud of it because I looked after myself and got through it in good nick. Towards the end of the run I went to see the nurse at the National Theatre. When I said I'd hurt my ribs she said that she'd expected to see me a lot sooner. She goes to see every show when it opens and calculates which actors are likely to get hurt. It was my first out-and-out lead and she said I'd done really well. My acting teacher used to say that actors aren't just actors, they're athletes. It's not about going for runs or lifting weights but managing your time is really important. I was able to give my all to the performance and still see my friends afterwards. I felt like I'd really gained control.

But the thing I'm proudest of, is that I said I wanted to be an actor and now I *am* an actor.

May 2016

Maria

"In my forties I feel I should be moving forwards and I need a kick"

I may be on the train to London again but this meeting marks a change of direction. All of the previous interviewees, though very different, have been young women in their twenties who know one another as friends or colleagues. I had wondered how long this pattern would last. It could conceivably have carried on like that but today's interview moves the chain into a new age group.

Susan has chosen the teacher who inspired her. In her introduction she says, "My dear friend Maria is a secondary school drama teacher but is on the cusp of making some big changes in her career. She's amazing and is the reason I'm an actor today."

It's now more than a year since I started the project and I'm getting used to asking people to tell me their stories. I meet Maria in the cafe at Foyles Bookshop in Charing Cross Road, get some tea *and then ask Maria to talk about the things that have led her to this mid-life place where having influenced so many young people, she is now wondering what to do next.*

How did you come to choose a life in drama, Maria?

I was an only child and grew up in Leeds. My background was very working class and I was quite shy but when I was at middle school I discovered that I had a big voice and liked being funny. Then at high school I had a part in a costume drama and tried to speak with a standard BBC accent. Glenda Jackson was on TV at the time playing Queen Elizabeth and there were these gorgeous Northern mums who came to the play and said, "Oooh, you sound just like Glenda Jackson." I liked that. I discovered stories through doing drama and they helped me to find my voice and feel powerful, so I decided that I wanted to be an actress. I knew, too, that drama would give me something I could use. I couldn't quite articulate what it was but I had a sense of responsibility to give something back. That came from my upbringing.

Later, when I was thinking about university, I knew that I wanted to come to London. As a child I'd read a lot of books that were set here and it seemed like you could disappear and be anything you wanted to be. I loved being in Leeds but I felt that I didn't belong. If I'd stayed then I would have had to keep within the norm. But I was the first person in my family to go to university and I suppose it gave me the ability to change things. I particularly liked the mix of people at Goldsmiths. They were from all different classes and there was a lot happening there politically so that's where I went. Because I'd grown up in the seventies I think I longed for a Ken Loach experience. There was an occupation going on—I can't even remember what it was about but I loved the idea of it.

What happened after you graduated?

Most people say that they fall into drama teaching and that's certainly what happened to me. I'd done some education projects and liked them, but then at the end of my degree I discovered I was having my son. And this was probably the biggest wake-up call and inspiration I could have had.

From then on I had to take him into account but I was excited when I heard about a postgraduate course in performance that was being run by English National Opera. I was able to do that because it was in the evening. So I went along three times a week and met fantastic people. There was lots of money for projects like that then and they trained me up to become a workshop facilitator, or animateur as it was rather pretentiously known. I'd be sent out with an opera singer and we'd work in schools and with community groups to put on an opera. And through the people I met and the skills I learned, I discovered that I loved facilitating.

What did you love about it?

It wasn't the opera. I'd had no experience of that when I was growing up. I didn't love opera before I did the course and by the end of it I still didn't. But it was a way of developing as a performer and I saw how it could reach out to kids. All those traditional stories are just variations on a theme. Whether it's the tragedies, the farce or the iconic characters, you can find ways to relate them to your life. One key moment was doing *Orpheus and Euridyce* with a group of kids from Bermondsey. We ran through fields in South East London and I remember thinking that this was an amazing experience and that something of it might stay with them.

The workshops led to me teaching at a Saturday school and gradually the performances became less opera-focused. By then I knew that I really liked making theatre with young people and that there was a purpose to it. I started to meet kids where I thought, "I know your story—it's not my story but I understand it and can see how drama can help you make a difference like I feel it helps me make a difference." Our culture now is very prescriptive so it's important that kids get the chance to express themselves. Some of the kids that come on a Saturday are not the high fliers or the ones that get picked for the school play but our sessions put them on a level playing field and they share experiences. It's a space that's theirs. And it's two-way—often they tell me about the books they're reading. It's that constant cycle of sharing that we're all going through all the time.

After a while of doing that I ended up working at a school in Stratford in East London and it changed my life in lots of ways. The head went on to become head of OFSTED. There was real quality right across that school. The boys were joined together as a community, almost like a brotherhood—there was such empathy between them. I saw something in their work that was quite humbling. Opera was outside their experience but they just embraced it because they trusted one another and they were kind and generous. I felt there was something very special happening there. And when I look back on the nineties it seems like more of a golden time in schools. Nowadays everything is very controlled. You get given less time and teachers often ask you to link your work to the curriculum. It affects what you can do creatively. There's a lot less freedom.

I've also spent some years teaching GCSE and A-Level drama in an independent school. I've done all sorts of different things. Sometimes I've done workshops and people have asked me to go back and do some other work. And that's how it's progressed—one thing leading on to another.

Where have your influences come from?

Something that really influenced me was working as a hospital cleaner in Leeds. It was a summer job and I've never forgotten the women that I worked with. They'd start cleaning the university at 5am, then they'd come and clean the hospital and then they'd go and clean the local bingo hall. They were strong and brave. I was rubbish at cleaning but they were so kind to me. They went on strike for better pay but they still continued to have integrity in doing their job. I've been very lucky in the work I've done in schools but the memory of those women has stayed with me, and reminds me that I want to make a difference to people who don't have a voice.

But I suppose that my son is my main inspiration. He's studying languages and is now in his last year at university. And as he's nearing the age that I was when I had him, I think he recognises that I might not have gone down the teaching route if I hadn't had him when I did. I don't see these things as sacrifices but he says, "Come on Mum, it's time for you now." He's really keen for me to be brave. I feel a commitment to him because of that belief. And also because of the kids I've taught, like Susan. You're continually telling them to go out into the world and be brave—to take a journey and have their Laurie Lee moment. Some of the kids I've taught have come back to help me as facilitators. One is a girl who trained at Royal Central School of Speech and Drama and she's way beyond me now. It's lovely to see this as you get older. But in my forties I feel that I should be moving forwards myself and that I need a kick. There's nothing worse than when someone you've taught asks, "Are you still there?"

For a long time I've been teaching GCSE and A-level and that's paid the bills and brought my son up. But now I'm at a point where I'm thinking, "OK Maria, you need to do something different." I'm getting those emotional, weepy feelings that everyone says you get in your forties. "Who am I? How have I changed from when I started out? Perhaps my skills aren't what I thought they were..."

So what are you going to do next?

I'm about to start a master's degree. I thought about doing something drama-related but instead I decided to do Children's Literature at Goldsmiths where I started. I've come full circle. I feel like Goldsmiths looked after me when I moved to London and now I'm going back there to be nourished again. I need to learn how to learn again, and to be challenged.

Why children's literature?

I really admire the course leader, Michael Rosen and the work he does in education. And a child's imagination is where it all starts. As an only child, I'd take out four books a day from the local library—things like Joan Aitken, and The Little House on the Prairie books. But it's interesting that people are quite confused when I say I'm not doing it to become a children's writer or anything else in particular. I love the idea of the people I'll meet and what we'll share but I don't necessarily see it going anywhere or that it will make me a better teacher. Mostly it's an indulgence and an adventure. I'm even enjoying thinking about the journey to get to New Cross from North London a few evenings a week. One thing is that I haven't been overzealous with the reading list and preparation. I'm just going to go and be open and see what happens—it feels exciting to do that. And it's an environment that I know. I think as you get older you become more aware that you're alone and it's all down to you. That's probably why I chose to go back to Goldsmiths as I feel safe there. It's a mad, bonkers place but it's great.

Did you always know that you wanted to study children's literature?

No not at all. Originally I wanted to act, but now I realise that it wouldn't have worked out. Acting is so hard and I don't think that I had what Susan's got, which is a lucky star—it's about being in the right place at the right time. It's possible that I have it now, but back then I'd have wasted a lot of time. With hindsight I can see that my son was the right thing for that time. If I hadn't had him I would have sat around not really doing anything, with my head up my backside. As it happened his father and I had lots of out-of-work friends who'd just graduated, and they helped to bring him up. There were the usual struggles but with a lot of my jobs I could take my son with me. It just kind of worked out. He inadvertently led me into the field of work I was meant to go to and young people have never failed to inspire and support me. Watching a group of young women produce an event for a charity *Justice for Care* was a recent humbling moment in my career. It was called *You Can't Arrest an Idea*. And along with colleagues I've met, I wouldn't be who I am if it wasn't for my son and the students I've worked with. This has turned out to be the most fantastic journey and I wouldn't change any of it.

September 2016

Helen

"That was one of the most devastating things I saw and it impacted very much on my feelings about how to support people at the end of their life"

I'm heading North at last. There's been quite a gap since I met Maria but she has passed me on to her old schoolfriend in Leeds and as I need to make a trip there anyway to research another piece of writing, I decide it's worth waiting until I can combine the two things. I could of course do the interview by video call but prefer to meet in person if at all possible.

Maria told me that Helen was always encouraging when they were at school together. She would say, "Yes of course you can do drama. Of course you can be an actress." Helen went into a very different kind of career. She became a nurse, and Maria tells me how much she admires her commitment to the NHS and the fact that "she just powers on in the face of adversity."

I've arranged to meet Helen in a cafe in the middle of Leeds. It's the end of the afternoon and I'm sure she's very busy but like all the other interviewees she is patient and engaged while I ask her to reflect on her life and influences. I have worried that I'm not offering anything in return for all this time they're giving me, other than the odd cup of tea, so I was really pleased to get an email from Maria shortly after our interview. She said that she'd found it a joy to sit and think about where she was in her life and what she wanted to do next. Perhaps they are getting something out of it after all. I'd like to think that.

Helen has some remarkable stories to tell and even though it's now over twenty years since she spent time working in the Romanian orphanages, her eyes fill with tears when she talks about some of the children she met. They are powerful memories and have shaped her approach to nursing.

What are you doing at the moment, Helen?

For the past few years I've been working as a clinical nurse specialist with malignant melanoma patients, and I love it. My role is varied and quite different from the usual sort of nursing. I act as a key worker in co-ordinating care but a big part of my work is offering psychological and emotional support to patients and their families. I meet people from all walks of life and follow them through until they're discharged or they die. Until about five years ago we had no real treatment for patients who had developed Stage 4 melanoma and the survival rate was very poor. But recently we've been trialling immunotherapy which involves stimulating the body's immune system so that it attacks the cancer. It's given intravenously in the chemotherapy day unit and the side effects are different from chemotherapy. People don't lose their hair and whilst they might get a bit of sickness, we're finding that many patients are able to carry on working full-time during their treatment. Other cancer groups are starting to use it too but we're still on a learning curve. It makes melanoma an exciting area to work in.

How did you get into nursing?

I always wanted to do it. If you'd asked me at five years old I would have said that I wanted to be a nurse. My mum was a physiotherapist, my grandad was a pharmacist, and four of my aunts were nurses or midwives. So I grew up hearing conversations about that kind of world and perhaps that sparked my interest. I think it's a personality thing too. Like Maria, I enjoyed drama and I did toy with the idea of that, but in the end I chose nursing.

I trained at Leeds General Infirmary in the days when they

took a new cohort of trainees every three months. There were about thirty-five of us and we had six weeks in the School of Health before starting our first ward placement. People now, would have a fit at what we did. We were certainly thrown in at the deep end. I was quite quickly exposed to seriously ill patients and assisting with things like cardiac arrests. You'd observe a procedure and then be told, "Nurse Jackson, that lady over there needs catheterising. Off you go—I'll watch you." So you did it and your confidence grew. And sometimes funny things happened. One day I was working with another student nurse and we were told to get a patient ready for a procedure so my colleague got a gown from the linen cupboard and went behind the curtains to dress the patient. I was talking to the staff nurse and then the curtains were pulled back and there was this little elderly lady in a frilly bedsheet kind of thing. She obviously knew what she was wearing but hadn't had the heart to say anything. It was a shroud. Fortunately she did see the funny side.

What did you do after you qualified?

Not long after qualifying I went to work in Romania as part of a charity based in Constanta on the Black Sea. It was about eighteen months after the revolution and I was on a ward for children with AIDS. It was very challenging and I saw things that no-one would ever want to see but it was as much a rewarding experience as a devastating one. They'd already had some help from charities so the situation was vastly improved from what it had been. But compared to what you would see here it was still like watching a car crash.

Under Ceausescu's regime both abortion and contraception were illegal. He'd wanted people to have as many children as possible in order to create a massive workforce but the trouble was that people were completely impoverished and huge numbers of children were abandoned. It was devastating for parents to leave their children at the orphanages but they simply couldn't afford to look after them. The orphanages had very few facilities and would typically have just two members of staff. It was a constant cycle of changing and feeding, and babies were left propped up in cots with bottles. The children were malnourished and many had anaemia. They also had deficits because no one was talking to them or stimulating them. Children who aren't picked up or cuddled will eventually stop crying.

Another problem was that paediatricians were desperate to keep children alive—if a child died, their wages were docked. This led to practices that you wouldn't even consider under normal circumstances. For example, the staff got the idea that if they gave children small infusions of blood then that would strengthen them. They'd get cheap blood from Africa and other places and give children between 10ml and 30ml each. One 450ml bag of blood goes quite a long way like that, and as they re-used syringes and needles, it resulted in a huge population of children with AIDS. At that time the country was closed to outside information but the doctor in charge of the hospital began to realise what was happening. She reported seeing large numbers of children with HIV and AIDS-related symptoms. The response from the Government was to ban her from talking about it or seeking help, and she was followed by the Securitate.

When the regime ended she could go to conferences and seek outside help but there was still no money for treatment. And the awful thing was that people were scared of these children.

When you got there what did you find?

By then, the children weren't just being left in their cots. There was a playroom with toys and a television and they were given meals. There were also some educational activities but the bathroom situation was dire. There were a couple of big toilets but these were no good for the little children so they had a row of potties. The kids all had chronic diarrhoea and the potties weren't emptied regularly. Once a week the children were washed—they were literally hosed down. We said that if we did nothing else then we wanted to provide a proper bathroom for them. We also built a playground on a bit of scrub grass. A lot of the children had joint problems because they'd been in cots for three years so they needed facilities where they could play and develop. My mum came over and did some physiotherapy with them. It was nice but can you imagine if people did that here? In Romania, they were so desperate for help that anyone could have wandered in.

Another thing that we tried to do was to boost the confidence and morale of the nursing staff. There was a stigma to working with these children and people didn't feel it was anything to be proud of. The staff were all poor and they didn't understand why so much care was being lavished on children who were going to die anyway. In this country we understand the need to support people through terminal illness—to give care and pain relief. But that concept wasn't there for them.

Did that change?

It started to. We did a lot of work with the staff. For example, a convoy came over with medical supplies and I asked for some nice things that we could give to the nurses. We made up a box for each of them with chocolate, coffee, soap—things to make them feel valued and that they couldn't afford to buy in the shops. There was also the problem that by coming in and doing things in the hospital, we were undermining them to a certain extent. It was like saying, "You haven't been doing your job well enough so other people are coming in to help you do it better." We wanted to avoid them feeling that.

There were many difficult things but one still really upsets me. It was not long after I got there, and a child came to the hospital from the orphanage. She was a little girl of about six although she looked much smaller, and she was skeletal and moribund. I went into one of the side rooms with another English nurse and found her there. It was clear that she was dying but she was all alone and grossly dehydrated. Her breathing was really laboured and she was very uncomfortable—I felt so angry. I went out of the room and collared one of the nurses who said, "Well she's dying. What can we do? There's no point."

The staff couldn't understand why we were so upset but we gave her some fluids and some Calpol—they did at least have that. And we just sat with her and she died in our arms not very long afterwards. When she did die, one of the nurses came in to light a candle. They do that when someone dies and they blow it out to let the spirit go. Then they literally bundle up the dead body in a sheet, tie it up at either end and swing it down the corridor to the mortuary. That was one of the most devastating things I saw and I think it has impacted very much on my feelings about how to support people at the end of their life. Here, I see some very upsetting things but however difficult it is, I don't see anything like that. There, life was cheap but hopefully my patients don't die in pain. You can't make it perfect every time because sometimes emergencies happen, but generally where you can, you try to make the end as supported and dignified as possible.

I also remember a little girl called Florentina who was three and a half. I liked her from the moment I saw her. She was very spirited and hilarious—a right little monkey. She used to run around and talk but then she got quite poorly with diarrhoea. She was in her cot and I asked if I could have some stuff to clean her up but they said, "She's already been changed today." And I said, "Yes, but she needs changing every ten minutes." So we cleaned her up and gave her some sips of water because she was grossly dehydrated. It was summer and about forty degrees. We gave her some mashed up food and she survived the whole process. After that she called me 'Mummy' and it was really hard to leave her when I came home. She was such a bright, lovely little thing and if she hadn't been born into that awful situation, she would have had lots to offer in life.

The hot water system in Romania was turned on and off by the Government so you would never know when you were going to get it. When I got back to England and was working in a hospital I remember turning on the taps, and being surprised that the water was warm, and also that there was so much in the drugs cupboards. In Romania we had very few basic medicines. Sometimes I think that if people could only see that then there would be a greater appreciation of what we do have. Some things are just too powerful to ever leave you.

What else has influenced the way you work today?

My parents divorced when I was ten and that was quite a defining moment. We moved from a little village in Hampshire to a challenging inner city area of Leeds. My mum had to be very tough because she was pregnant when my dad left. The role of being supportive started early on—there are five of us and I'm the eldest—and I felt responsible for my siblings and also for my mum as I could see that she was very sad. My grandmother took us in and later when my mum bought a house she moved in with us. She was like a second mum and did lots for all of us—she was an amazing lady. She had cancer when I was nineteen and as my mum has no brothers or sisters, I was the only person there to help. My mum and I got to the hospital just a few minutes after she died. It was very early in the morning so when we came back home, the other kids were in bed. And I could see that my mum wouldn't be able to tell them. So I told the boys and then I told the girls. It was devastating but I did it.

That was my first experience of breaking bad news and I do it rather a lot now. I suppose it's been a pattern in my career—if ever relatives have needed to be phoned then nine times out of ten people say, "Helen will you do it?" and I think it's because I understand. It's a huge responsibility. People may not remember what you said or what you did but they'll remember how you made them feel at that moment. It's important to be really honest. But I think people also need to feel that you care about the person that was important to them. You need to make it personal and not as if you're reading it from a sheet. I always try to think that if this was my husband or brother or sister how would I like to be told. What would be the important things for me to hear? If any of my patients are dying in the hospital then I'll often go to see the family during that time or just after. Because I've known their relative for some time then I can talk to the family in a different way. Sometimes you don't have to say very much. It's just about holding someone and letting them talk about their relative. And being an anchor when everything has gone haywire.

What are the best and worst bits of your job?

Sometimes the worst and the best bits come together. It's an enormous privilege to look after people when they're facing challenges and are at their most vulnerable. You get to know your patients and whilst you treat them all the same, there will always be people that you particularly connect with. It's hugely rewarding to support people through a difficult process but when you watch them deteriorate and die it can be very hard. You have to remember that it's not your relative but equally as a human being it's impossible not to relate to that. Whatever level of professionalism you maintain at work you still feel it and to say that I never shed tears over my patients would be a lie. I absolutely do, and sometimes with them, but you learn ways of coping because otherwise you couldn't do it. The uniform is a kind of armour—you do your work and then you take it off. I get the bus to and from work and that forty-five minutes at the end of the day is like a psychic shower. I read a book or I think and then when I walk through the door at home, that's it. But the day I don't find my job a privilege is the day I think I should leave. I don't ever feel that I made the wrong decision. I still love what I do.

February 2017

Liz

"I first went to India in 1985 and I just knew there would be more to it than a holiday"

I'm in the North again. This time it's York and it's lucky that as before I've been able to combine this interview with a research trip.

Helen has chosen her Mum's friend as the next link. Liz is a physiotherapist and it was her example of volunteering in India that inspired Helen to look into volunteering herself. That was how she found herself in Romania.

I've had several email exchanges with Liz and she thoughtfully sent a link to a photo of her on the website of a local church where she is a deacon. So when I arrive at the Waterstones cafe in the city centre I know that I need to look out for a woman with short grey hair and a big smile. She's there on time wearing a smart jacket and a friendly but slightly hesitant look. I need to remind myself each time that while I have a rough format for the interview, my interviewee has no idea what I'm going to ask.

We find a quiet corner and it's mid-morning so I join the queue for coffee and cake. That takes a while, but once we get settled I hear for the first time in this project from someone who can look back from a busy post-retirement life on a long, successful career.

How did you get into physiotherapy, Liz?

I wanted to be a physiotherapist from when I was thirteen. I don't know where it came from really. I just wanted to do it and I've absolutely loved it. It's been the most wonderful career and it's taken me to many countries.

How did the travel come about?

My first taste of international work was in 1973 when I won a Winston Churchill Travel Fellowship. These awards were set up when Winston Churchill died and provide marvellous opportunities for people from all backgrounds to travel, research particular subjects and share their knowledge. I wanted to look at new techniques for treating children with neurological conditions, particularly cerebral palsy, and I had a month each in Hungary, Switzerland and Italy. Hungary was particularly interesting because it was in the middle of the Cold War. I tried to make personal contacts before I went so that people would trust me and I found a lovely man to teach me some Hungarian. He had left Hungary in 1956 and was working as a book illustrator at York University. He cried because he was so delighted that someone wanted to learn his language.

When I got to Hungary I found that people wanted to talk. Sometimes I'd be sitting on a bus next to someone and as we went into a tunnel and there was a lot of noise they'd start whispering in my ear. Things that they didn't want to be overheard—criticisms about the system. And one day I dropped a book in the park and an elderly lady picked it up. "Are you English?" she said and then she took me round to various places. One was a radio station in the hills above

Budapest. It was manned by Russian guards with huge Alsatian dogs patrolling the perimeter and she started shouting all sorts of anti-Russian things. She was delighted to practise her English and was afraid of nothing. She turned round from shouting at the Russians and said, "My dear, do you have good bread in England?" Given the shortages they had to endure, that was quite poignant.

I focused on Conductive Education while I was in Hungary. This helps neurologically impaired children to have as much independence as possible without resource to special equipment and aids. It brings together education, psychology and therapy approaches to unlock potential. Sometimes the criticism has been that they had to use that system because they didn't have resources. Also that there was absolutely nothing before and the children stayed in bed for months. Those things are probably true, but nonetheless I saw children making enormous progress. There was something magical there about the holistic approach they used and the way that they did things like linking movement to language.

Then I had a month in Bern, Switzerland and that was very different. Physiotherapists using the Bobath approach were treating children who were born with an identifiable neurological problem and that was almost ten per cent of the neonatal population. They believed that if you started really early you could make a huge difference. But that level of care is not sustainable in most countries and I think they were promising more than they could achieve. Nonetheless, I learned a huge amount. Today, it's evidence-based practice that's the thing.

I was given £1,012 for my travel fellowship. It was a lot of money in those days and it took the whole of my lunch hour to sign for it at the bank. I didn't spend it all and so when I came home, I sent two hundred pounds back. The secretary was lovely and said, "Oh dear! Have you been eating enough?"

My travel fellowship started me off on an international path and it just grew. I never really set out to do that.

So what happened next?

I worked at the hospital here in York for twenty wonderful years—everyone in the team was doing something at national level so it was very vibrant. We started getting visitors coming to look at our work and as the international interest grew I began to feel restless. Then a friend invited me to go on holiday to India where he'd lived for a year as one of the Brothers of Charity. He said, "I'd like to take you back to where I used to live, and show you India. Would you like to come?" I thought, "No, I wouldn't, what a terrifying idea"—and so I said "OK!"

That was in 1985 and I just knew there would be more to it than a holiday. I couldn't sleep the night before we flew—my mouth was dry and my heart was pounding. Anyway, we arrived in Calcutta in the middle of the monsoon at midnight. People were bustling and shouting and pulling at my suitcase. They were all telling me to get into their cars which probably weren't even proper taxis. It was such an assault on the senses. Even now that I've been back many times, I still find it's like that.

We went and spent about a week at the Home for the Dying. I'd love to have met Mother Theresa but she was in Ethiopia at the time. One of the things I will never forget was watching a young Japanese girl. She was only about eighteen and was sitting with a lady who was dying. They had no shared language, and anyway the lady was too ill to say much.

But somehow the girl communicated and looked after her. She was so observant and responsive—she loved her to the end and it was beautiful. She seemed to epitomise what the place was about. She's wasn't very old but she just *got* it. I found that deeply moving.

From there we went on to Delhi. I'd noticed a job offer in our physiotherapy journal but I didn't take the details with me because I wasn't thinking it would be relevant to me. And then my friend said, "Why don't you go and see them?" and I said, "I don't know where they are—I don't have the address," thinking to myself, "I'm off the hook." But what happened next was very surprising. We were sitting in a taxi doing some sightseeing when a van stopped next to us. On the side it said *Spastics Society of Northern India* with the address and everything I needed to know, though thankfully the name has changed now. So I took it as a sign—I went along and spoke to the receptionist and she said, "We're very busy today and can't see anybody." So I thought, "Oh good, I'm off the hook again." But then to my horror as I was walking out, I heard footsteps behind me and someone said, "Did you say you're British?" I said, "Yes" and she said, "The director will see you."

So I went in to see the director of the centre and it was extraordinary. She said, "We haven't had anyone respond to this advert and I've just been praying that someone would walk in off the street." I thought, "Oh my goodness me, I don't think I'm off the hook at all."And when she said, "I think you'll fit in quite well here," I felt a mixture of relief and dread. For the past two years I'd been giving up lots of things that I did in my spare time but without knowing why. And as a person of faith I saw it as God needing to dig me up because York had become a bit of a tap root. It took a year to sort out the bureaucracy and funding but when I went back to India, I stayed for three years and have continued to visit since.

How did it work out?

Seeing the poverty was a challenge. I think that's why I felt so ambivalent about going to India in the first place—it's such a spectrum. You do what you can but the problems are so enormous that they can drag you down. Some years later, I remember being asked to go and visit a family in a village in Andhra Pradesh. I went with two colleagues and we got there quite late in the evening. It was dark and we bent low to get into the family's hut which was very basic. There was one light bulb swinging from the ceiling and we saw a young boy who had clearly got muscular dystrophy. His father was very anxious and was desperate to know what he could do for him. We asked if he had any other children and he said that he had another two. They were outside and when we looked, we could see that they were in the earlier stages of the disease—one of them was not able to run and the other was just sitting on the floor, very still. I shall never forget those three children and the father wanting us to help. There were no resources and all we could tell him was to try as far as possible to give his children the same experiences as other children in the village. And to love them. My colleagues and I went back to the car and cried.

You can't solve that problem here, either, but you can make the journey from disability to the end of life, much better. And even in limited circumstances small things can make a difference. I remember a young boy of about fourteen who came to the Delhi centre with his family. He had muscular dystrophy, too, and couldn't move much. He'd been lying flat on the floor and was terrified of drowning when he had a drink. So we propped him up on a bean bag and gave him a straw. It was such a simple thing but he was so relieved.

It takes time to train physios, and sometimes you simply need more pairs of hands so we tried to make it easier for people to become competent. I worked closely with a very skilled Indian occupational therapist who became a good friend. We found people who were interested in working with disabled children and then we taught them everything we knew about paediatrics. In some cases, they actually ended up knowing more about children with disabilities than the people who'd been through university. They were such a great group of people—some of them went off and set up charities of their own and I'm so proud of them. That wouldn't have happened so quickly if we'd gone down the regular route.

There have been massive changes since my first visit to India. Then, I'd be greeted at the local store by a man in a white coat who would say, "Good morning Madam," and write down what I bought in a ledger. It had a lovely Indian carpet on the floor. Now it's a supermarket selling ready meals.

Things are hugely more prosperous, but the problem is in making sure that development reaches the poorer sectors of society.

And what else did you do?

After my time in India, I spent four years as a consultant physiotherapist working in a number of countries including Mauritius, Vietnam, Yemen, Kenya and Zambia. Then I became the international development adviser to the Chartered Society of Physiotherapy (CSP) and that meant I could help other people who were wanting to go and work abroad, like me.

I also became so interested in trying to understand other cultures that I did a degree in anthropology. It was good but I felt like I asked more and more questions and got fewer and fewer answers.

Then I did some work in the EU with physiotherapy colleagues from several member countries. It was about checking up on EU health legislation to see how it would affect the profession and also promoting the professional standards set by the World Confederation for Physical Therapy. We sometimes went to speak to health ministers and said, "This is the standard that we're working to in Europe. How do you think you could help promote this?" For example, we had a twinning partnership with the Czech physio association. I believe in collaboration and sensible communication. Tremendous good has been done in Brussels so I'm finding the present Brexit situation a bit difficult.

In 2010, the year I retired, I got an award from the World Confederation for Physical Therapy. It was for international practice and such an honour to get that from my colleagues. That was wonderful!

What are you doing now that you've retired from physiotherapy?

I was ordained into the Church of England in 2009 and don't feel called to the priesthood but I do feel called to being out in the community. So I'm a vocational deacon. As well as being involved in all the usual church things like children's work and preaching, I'm chaplain to the businesses in our parish, and I'm part of the chaplaincy team at York Racecourse. I also do Street Angels which is run by a group of churches in York. We help people who've been out partying—they're quite vulnerable if they've over-indulged. There are often young girls who find their shoes a bit of a challenge, so we give out water and flip flops and make sure they get home safely—I meet all sorts of people doing that and enjoy it a lot.

And I've just come back from a three-month sabbatical. I decided to make a list of people that I love and I came up with forty-three. I didn't manage to get round them all but I did quite well. I ended up visiting Holland, Scotland, Germany and Estonia. It did make me feel really refreshed and I think sometimes when you're busy and doing a lot of things you can forget about yourself. So that was a good reminder that I need to factor in a bit more time for me. Other people have been telling me that for quite a while.

June 2017

Gareth

"I lived in Kabul and we were not there to be heroic—
we were there with a purpose"

It can't have escaped anyone's notice having read this far, that the first eight interviewees have been women. I've not steered it that way, and have in fact been very careful **not** *to influence any of the interviewee's choices. But the fact that women have consistently passed me on to other women, has made me wonder whether I should from now on, instruct the interviewees to carry on doing this so that it becomes a defining characteristic—an all-female chain. I considered this for a while but then remembered how my original hope had been to collect a variety of stories, and that I can best do this by talking to all kinds of people. So I decided to stick with the non-interventionist approach and then Liz passed me on to Gareth which resolved the issue once and for all.*

She had already referred to him in our interview, although not by name. He was the friend who invited her to go on holiday to India, and as she said, "That was the start of amazing things for me." Gareth is now a vicar and Liz says that "he is pretty much the most inspirational person I know." Like Susan and Helen, Liz has chosen someone who has had a profound influence on the course of her life, and it's pleasing to see these connections.

I drive to Gareth's vicarage, about an hour away. He has promised to 'have the kettle on' for my arrival and duly welcomes me with tea and biscuits. The morning sun streams into his study where we sit surrounded by books, paperwork and clocks.

Gareth starts by describing himself modestly as 'just an ordinary common or garden vicar working in the Church of England.' But as he goes on to talk about his experiences of working overseas and the path that led him to ordination, it becomes clear that he has had an extraordinary life. Not many 'common or garden vicars' have lived in Kabul under the Taliban regime.

What are you doing at the moment, Gareth?

I've been the vicar of this parish for about four and a half years and have been ordained for twelve years. I carry out Sunday services, midweek services, baptisms, weddings and lots of funerals. I'm also involved with a number of local schools and do assemblies. Once or twice a week I go to a local childrens' hospice where I'm chaplain and I always take my Labrador, Libby with me. People aren't necessarily interested in seeing a vicar but they're always interested in seeing a Labrador. It doesn't take a huge amount of my time but it's an important aspect of local involvement.

What led you to become ordained?

I was raised in the 1960s when it was not uncommon for children to go to church and Sunday school. I remember having a simple childlike faith but not necessarily feeling that it made a personal difference to my own life. And then when I was twelve I was involved in a serious car crash. I was waiting for a bus when a drunken driver veered across the road and ploughed into the bus shelter. The person on one side of me was disabled for life and the person on the other side was killed. Both my legs were broken and I ended up in hospital. That gave me time to reflect on faith, life and death in a way that would normally be unusual for a twelve-year old. Six months later I went to an evangelical meeting and people were invited to come forward and dedicate their lives to God. I remember thinking, "Yes, this matters to me and I want to make this commitment." The person who was speaking said, "This shouldn't be just a phase or a fad—a commitment to God is something that should be life changing." As I went forward I thought, "What I'm doing now will impact on the rest of my life." And indeed it has—in ways both good and troubling.

When you said that you made a commitment what did that mean to you?

I knew that my understanding of the Christian faith was limited and childlike in many respects but I found a way of love profoundly attractive and wanted to replicate it in my own life. As a Christian one does not have to be ultra-ascetic but I do think it's about learning to live simply and to place value on relationships, key values and ethical principles rather than material things. As a child I could not articulate that but I did feel very drawn to it even though that now feels quite countercultural.

So what happened next?

I got involved in the local church youth group and then went off to university to study politics. I wasn't altogether sure what to do after that—I considered ordination but was told that it's good to get some experience of life first. So after I graduated in 1981 I decided to take a year out. It was shortly after Mother Theresa had won the Nobel Peace Prize and rather naively I thought that it would be interesting to go and work with her and her organisation. I discovered that there's a male order called the Missionary Brothers of Charity that works with her Sisters, and that you can go and be a volunteer. So I went off to join them. It seems very naïve now but I just booked a one-way ticket to Calcutta. I was twenty-one and arrived at the airport with a few travellers' cheques and an address. When I got to the Brothers' house it turned out that they hadn't received my letter but they were incredibly welcoming and I ended up staying with them for about a year. I didn't stay in Calcutta all that time as they thought it would be interesting for me to see some other places. So for a number of months I worked with their mobile leprosy clinic in the state of Bihar in Northern India. I had no medical skills or anything really, but they were very gracious.

I'd obviously read about leprosy in the Bible but although it has been almost eradicated in most of the world it does still exist in some parts. I remember seeing people whose noses had disappeared and whose hands were reduced to stumps. They often had terrible sores because Hansen's Disease (its proper name) kills the nerve endings. People have no sense of pain and cause themselves terrible injuries by doing things like picking up boiling pots. I also heard stories about people having the stump ends of their feet chewed at night by rats but not waking up because they couldn't feel it. I worked in the pharmacy part of the clinic and would count the tablets and give them out in little screws of paper. One of the biggest challenges was getting people to take the full course of treatment. Their symptoms would partially improve and so they'd stop taking the medicine. From talking to the Brothers I began to understand some of the challenges faced by people in that part of the world. They would have to walk for two or three days to get to the clinic, and then another two or three days back to their village. It was difficult for them to take that time away from tending their land.

There was one incident that I particularly remember. We were on our way to set up the clinic for the day when a child ran out from the side of the road. There was nothing the driver could do and we hit it with our jeep. My first thought was "OK, we're in a jeep ambulance that's marked with a red cross, so we'll stop and take the child to hospital." But I was staggered when the Brothers started locking the doors and the jeep sped off. I remonstrated with the driver and said that we should stop. But the Brothers said, "If we do that, there'll be a mob reaction—the villagers will force us out of the jeep and they might set light to it in revenge. Instead we must go straight to the next village, turn ourselves in to the police and explain what has happened." So that's what we did—it was about five miles away. We hid the jeep round the back and a policeman stood guard over it while we went into the police station and there was lots of explanation in Hindi. I asked, "What happens now?" and they said, "The villagers will come to the police station." Sure enough a bit later on, various family members arrived with the child, having flagged down the next vehicle that came along. There was lots of shouting and then a process of negotiation. The child had some injuries but they weren't life threatening so it was agreed that we would take the family and the child to the local hospital and would pay for any treatment that was needed. It made me reflect on the fact that as a twenty-one year old white person, I was saying, "We need to do the right thing." But as a foreigner I knew nothing about how these things work.

What did you do at the end of that year in India?

I did some trekking in Nepal and then came back to the UK. I worked in London for a while in an administrative role at The Arts Council of Great Britain, in the HR department, where, among other roles, I served as editor of their in-house magazine. But by then, my exposure to Asia and the developing world was such that I wanted in that clichéd phrase, *to make a difference.*

I also wanted to understand more about *good development* because you can both help and hinder. I didn't have a science O-Level to my name so there was no way I was going to be a medic but I knew that health service management is important and managed to get a place on the NHS National Management Training Scheme. I spent two years in Yorkshire learning about health services management and then applied to work with a Christian development organisation in Nepal. They've been working in that region since 1852 so had lots of cultural understanding and experience. I went out as an HR manager and eventually became the HR director. At that time they were one of the largest employers in the country, second only to the Government, with many thousands of Nepali staff and over four hundred expats.

Our remit was to deliver projects that would assist in the development of Nepal and its people. They spanned four main areas—engineering and industrial development, health, education, and rural development. The idea was to set them up and then train Nepali people to run them. The agreements forbade any overt proselytising but we aimed to work *in the name and spirit of Jesus Christ.*

So, for example in the hospitals and community health clinics which the mission helped to run, we sought to challenge traditional approaches and superstition but without undermining the local culture. For most people confronted with a problem such as epilepsy, their first recourse would be to a local jhankri or traditional healer. There were many thousands of these in the rural areas and far fewer Western-trained doctors. These traditional healers would use all sorts of practices that we might regard as somewhat suspect. But they are people of high status in their community and you would not want to alienate them. So rather than working against the local healers, the mission's Mental Health Programme tried to work with them and help them not to feel threatened by Western medicine. One of the things that worked well was running workshops where we trained them to identify some of the most common mental health problems.

We also worked on some big engineering projects such as hydropower schemes. Bringing electrical power to the villages had all kinds of knock-on benefits—people no longer had to cut down trees to burn and so this helped to stop the deforestation which leads to landslides and flooding.

Can you tell me about your time in Afghanistan?

I was asked to go there as HR Director to the International Assistance Mission which employed about five hundred Afghan staff and about a hundred expats. It was during a particularly unstable period in the early 1990s. Soviet troops had invaded in 1979 but left by 1989 and that led to the fall of the Russian-backed government. The West had worked assiduously to put the Pakistan-based mujahideen into power but within about six months, that government collapsed and broke up into a collection of different groups. After several years of internecine warfare, the Taliban came to power.

I lived in Kabul and it faced extraordinary destruction. On a bad day there might be two thousand shells and rockets landing in the city, and on a good day there might be only three or four hundred. There was continual upheaval and you always had to be ready to move with just one or two suitcases. I moved house eleven times in eighteen months. A couple of my friends were held with knives to their throats in the counteroffensive and a house where I lived was looted at gunpoint.

It was a fascinating time—very on-edge. During the day we went out to make sure our projects were functioning but at night it was often safest to be underground. There was one ten-week period when I slept in a basement with eight people from my mission. That was such a bonding experience that even now I'm still in touch with most of them. We sign off our emails as *Your BB*—Basement Buddy. They were extraordinary times and I'm grateful to have seen what was possible, even under fire. We were not there to be heroic, we were there with a purpose and our development projects were able to continue even though that sometimes meant being in a reduced form. At one stage during the Taliban era we were running pretty much the only mother and child health clinic in the whole of Kabul. That was pretty important.

What was the impact of the Taliban regime on women and children?

It was a country that had experienced quite considerable development in the past—when I give talks I often ask, "Who got the vote first? Was it Afghan women or Swiss women?" People are usually surprised to hear that it was Afghan women in 1964—Swiss women only got the vote in 1970! In the period prior to, and then during, the Soviet occupation, women held a huge number of significant jobs in areas like medicine, teaching and the Civil Service. But of course all of that went awry under the Taliban and it was a terrible shock for women to find their lives so limited. Many were already suffering mental health issues as a result of seeing people killed and they faced further trauma by being constrained to their homes.

Interestingly though, there is evidence to suggest that in

some respects, things got slightly better for women at that time. This seems counterintuitive but it was because the majority of qualified teachers had been women. As they were no longer allowed to work, it meant that boys tended to be educated in huge groups—perhaps a hundred in one class with just one male teacher giving a pretty appalling kind of rote learning education. On the other hand, women who were qualified teachers were keen to see education continue and so all across Kabul there was an extraordinary network of secret home schools for girls. Burka-clad women scurried from one alley to another without the Taliban realising what was going on. There would be up to fifteen girls in a class with one or two teachers and so some girls got a better education than the boys. And even in spite of the restrictions there were times when the Taliban had to accept that women had skills that they needed. So for example, the 400-bed military hospital in Kabul was run by an excellent trauma surgeon called Suhaila Seddiqi who held the rank of General in the Afghan Army. The Taliban tried to stop her working and then realised that they couldn't run the hospital without her so she carried on. She was always known as *General Suhaila* and when the Taliban fell she became Minister of Health.

What happened when you left Kabul?

After about three years in Kabul I came back to the UK and did a masters degree in post-war recovery studies. I was planning to go on and do a PhD but instead I found myself exploring ordination again, and that's when I went off to Cambridge to study theology.

You said earlier that the commitment you made was *full of blessings but also troubles*. What did you mean?

I guess I said that because I'm gay. When I was much younger I had a conservative view of that particular issue and the Christian approach to it. It led me to believe that the only option for a person in my situation was lifelong celibacy. And so I have lived an entirely celibate life but that view is not one I actually believe in any more—it's not one I would ever teach. Although it's quite a strong word to use, I think it's abusive of people and their personal integrity. I would never endorse a life style that's promiscuous but I'm entirely comfortable with same-sex marriage based on faithful, stable, monogamous relationships, and same-sex parenting. I've observed that at close quarters with a number of friends in same-sex relationships including those who have adopted children and have seen them doing an amazing job.

My hesitancy in my own life is because I still function in what can feel like quite a conservative environment within the Church. I probably work for the only employer in the UK that is entitled to sack me for that issue, which is bizarre when you think even the Armed Forces, which one might think of as traditionally homophobic, are now equal opportunity employers, but not the Church of England! I think if I had been born thirty years later, I might have made different choices. Faith would have been important to me but I don't think I would have ruled out the possibility of a relationship and I would love to have been a parent. My life story has been as it is and it's important to live life without regrets, but that's what was behind my ambivalence.

What are you most pleased to have done?

It's been fascinating to have experienced such diversity across continents and cultures, and I've made friends all over the world. But there are times when I see friends post pictures on Facebook of themselves with their first grandchild or with their husband or wife, and it makes me feel slightly wistful about what might have been. There's a temptation sometimes to wonder what I've achieved but I hope that I've modelled something of the love of God in the variety of contexts in which I've lived. I've wanted to be there for people at times of extraordinary difficulty as well as at times of great joy and thanksgiving. That's what I set out to do right from the beginning.

August 2017

Lesley

"The traumas were awful things that I would never wish on anyone and yet incomprehensibly out of them, amazing things have happened"

Gareth passes me on to Lesley and provides more background information than I usually get. She, like him, is ordained and works as a vicar in the Church of England. He studied with her sister, so knew of her many years ago but they met later through mutual friends and have been friends themselves for over ten years. He tells me that Lesley is the only British-born widow of the Rwandan Genocide and he promises that I'll find her interesting and inspiring.

At her urban vicarage, Lesley welcomes me warmly. She shows me into her cool, calm sitting room and goes off to the kitchen to make me a cup of tea.

I know very little about the Rwandan genocide and feel rather ashamed that when it was happening I was tied up in my own small world, busy raising my children. But I know enough to understand that Lesley's story will not be easy to hear and certainly not easy for her to tell. She has clearly recounted it many times before, including writing several books and taking part in TV programmes. That can never make something so horrific, easy to discuss particularly with a stranger and we stop several times while she gathers herself.

By the end I feel immensely privileged to have had this time with Lesley and indebted that she has been so open. She sends me off with biscuits for my journey, and we hug on the doorstep. Later she writes to say that she had been anxious before I arrived because she'd done interviews in the past and didn't want to end up "trotting out the same stuff again." In the event she realised that her life had moved on. "It was surprisingly helpful," she wrote. "It helped me realise what's really important in my life, and what I feel passionately about communicating to others. Thank you for letting me share my story! I was exhausted afterwards, but that didn't matter."

What does your work involve, Lesley?

It's a very mixed area here and St Andrew's Church is representative of that. It's quite a busy place. As well as church services we run groups for elderly people and children, a homeless project and a community cafe. There's lots of coming and going because we also rent out space to a charity that helps children get into college or university, and to other groups like the Scouts, dance classes and slimming clubs. Another part of our work is supporting people on two local housing estates. They've been living with the threat of demolition for over ten years so we've appointed a full-time youth and community worker who does support work and builds relationships with young people and families. In all the things we do here, I want people to know that our church is a place where they are welcome.

What led you to be a vicar?

Well, that's quite a long story. I was born and brought up in Scotland as the youngest of four. My dad was a Bible class teacher so we went to church but I had a mixed relationship with it and left in my early teens. Then when I was fifteen, I went to a youth camp and that was a real turning point. As the week went on I listened to people telling their stories and I became aware of the need to commit my life to God. I was terribly moved by having this sense of how I wanted to live my life and I came back very ardent—I think I must have driven people up the wall.

I was quite shielded in my upbringing but it was later at university that I started to become aware of the suffering in the world, and some of the inequalities. It seemed so unfair that we have everything we need but other places have so little. I wanted to do something useful and then one day after church I got the chance to chat with a chap from Tearfund. "I've got a French degree," I said. "What can I do?" And his advice was to get some vocational skills. So I moved to London and for the next three years, I did my nursing training. At the end I met a missionary doctor from a village hospital in Rwanda and asked if I could work with him. "Yes," he said, "if you pay for your flight and are willing to turn your hand to anything, we can find jobs for you to do." So off I went to Rwanda.

What was it like?

I had this idea that I was going out to be a pioneer but in many ways what I found was a fairly normal set-up. There was a hospital, a church, a couple of schools, and a little pocket of ex-pat professionals. But in other ways it was very different and the conditions on the ward were extremely basic. The floors were concrete and the toilets were pit latrines. The patients had a bed and a mattress but they'd bring their own sheets if they had them, because we didn't always have enough. They'd also bring a carer who would sleep on a mat under their bed at night. The carers did all the washing and feeding, and they'd cook their own food on open fires outside. It was very rural and there were wild dogs scavenging around. One very surprising thing was that the drugs weren't locked up like they would be in the UK—instead it was the linen that was closely guarded. As nurses, we did things like dressings and putting up drips. I was thrown in at the deep end and remember being terrified. But by the end of my six weeks there, I knew that I wanted to go back.

And did you manage to?

I did go back to that village and had a job with Tearfund. But first I did my midwifery training as I felt that I needed more skills. When I went back some of the work was in the hospital but a lot of it was out in the hills. I worked closely with a couple of colleagues, particularly a very competent Rwandan social worker called Anatolie. We would pack up our truck with vaccines, a medicine chest, water, soap, a mat for the pregnant women to lie on, and baby-weighing scales that we'd hang from a tree. Then we'd head out for maybe an hour or so, and set up our clinic. We'd visit each place about once a month and people would walk from miles around, carrying their babies on their backs with umbrellas to keep off the sun. If I thought women were at risk of a difficult birth then I'd tell them to come to the hospital. But often they wouldn't because if they were away there would be no-one to look after the children and the home, and do the work in the fields. Also, if they came to the hospital they would need to bring a carer to look after them. So they'd tend to wait till the last minute and then they'd go into labour and not be able to get to the hospital because it was so far away. It was very tough for these women and the infant mortality rate was quite high.

Another part of our work was running a community health programme. The communities in the hills around us each elected a health worker and we trained them in basic health and hygiene. They'd go out into their communities and tell people about things like washing their hands, keeping flies off food, digging proper toilets, and vaccinations. They'd also encourage them to vary their diet by growing some cabbages or tomatoes perhaps, rather then just eating beans and cooking bananas. Anatolie and I would go out from time to time and follow up with any families who needed extra advice. We'd drive off and after a while, Anatolie would say, "I think it's roughly about here." If we weren't sure of the way, we'd stop and in seconds we'd be surrounded by children. A car driving along the rough roads was a rare sight. "Do you know where so-and-so lives?" we'd ask, and they'd usually say, "Yes," and jump in the car to show us the way. They'd be so excited to get a ride.

Often, we'd walk for miles going from house to house, talking with people and sitting on rush mats outside their homes. I let Anatolie do a lot of the talking because it's a deferential culture—if I came in as an outsider and a white person, people would say, "Oh yes, yes, of course we'll do that. Yes we have this." Whereas Anatolie would say, "I know very well that you don't have that. I've been brought up in just the same way as you. Come on, let's go and have a look." She had a lovely way with people.

For us, it was actually a very healthy life. We were outside a lot and we ate a basic diet of beans, rice, cooking bananas, sweet potatoes, and a few other vegetables if we were lucky. We only had meat occasionally and there was nothing in the way of sweet stuff. Conditions at home were also basic. We only had electricity for three hours in the evening when the generator ran but that didn't always work so we used candles and paraffin lamps a lot. Our fridge also ran on paraffin and you had to remember to trim the wick or you would come back home and find the house full of disgusting black smoke. Food would go off quickly because it was so hot, and we often didn't have running water because the pump in the lake wasn't reliable.

Was it a happy time?

In some ways it was an incredibly fulfilling and happy time. But it could also be extremely lonely. For a long time I couldn't communicate at a *heart* level in the local language Kinyarwanda, and so I was restricted to the expat community. Sometimes that was great and sometimes it wasn't so good. I was conscious that there was a division between the locals and the expats and I didn't like that so I asked if I could go and live with a Rwandan family—I wanted to break down some of the barriers. And that was wonderful. They spoke only Kinyarwanda to me and they treated me like a daughter. Instead of saying, "Come and have the best seat," they'd say, "Come on—take your turn in the kitchen," and that was just what I wanted. I came to think of them as my Rwandan family.

The few Rwandans who spoke English were those who had lived abroad so I tended to socialise with them, and gradually I got to know more people. One of these was a chap called Charles. He was Rwandan but had been brought up in Uganda and studied in Kenya. He was a lovely young man. We met quite a lot in other people's homes and at church, and I became very fond of him. I thought initially that he was earmarked to marry somebody—but that didn't work out. Then he invited me out for a meal. We met in the capital Kigali and that was the beginning of our friendship. People don't really do *dates* in Rwanda. What happens is that a man decides what he's looking for in a wife. Things like being reasonably intelligent, able to cook and look after his visitors, good-looking or whatever, and then people will recommend a young woman. They'll meet once or twice in a communal context with the woman not necessarily knowing what everyone has in mind and then the man might say, "You're the one I want to marry."

So, after Charles and I had been out together, perhaps two or three times, he said, "You're the one I am going to marry." And I said, "Whoa...hang on! Do I get any say in this?" I thought that we needed to spend more time together. But that's difficult in Rwanda as it's not culturally appropriate. Anyway, to cut a long story short, we eventually decided to get married and had a traditional village wedding at the end of 1992. My husband's tribe the Tutsis are cattle people so cows played a part in the wedding. When a man wants to get married then his family has to negotiate with the woman's family and they decide what to give in exchange for her. Charles did all of this in a kind of symbolic way but it still involved his family and my Rwandan family doing some negotiation. They settled on one cow in exchange for me and another one to keep it company! At the wedding we were in the enclosure outside my Rwandan family's home and the two cows were paraded in. They had great long horns and the women sang to them. Then a cow expert came and inspected them. The whole ceremony was absolutely fascinating and after that we had a church wedding in the capital.

What was it like once you settled into life together?

It was lovely to be married but things were not ideal. One of Charles's nephews came to live with us, and then before long I began to notice that Charles had changed. Obviously I'd never been in a married relationship in Rwanda before, so there was a lot I didn't understand. The man is the head of the household and doesn't necessarily need to consult his wife about what he does. So Charles would often be out late and if I asked where he'd been, he'd say that he was visiting friends and that it wasn't any of my business. He said that if he had to tell me everything then people would see that as a sign of weakness. I was very confused and distressed. And all this time the political situation was getting more and more tense. There were rumours of massacres and at one point Charles thought that all his family had been wiped out. Even though we discovered that wasn't the case, it was still pretty horrible.

Then one day I had a visit from two local ladies. They sat me down and said, "We are sorry to tell you but your husband is having an affair." I said, "What? Of course he's not. When he's not here, he's down at the school, working." And they said, "No, he's not. He's at a woman's house." So that threw my whole world into turmoil and I realised it made sense and explained why he'd been so aloof. I challenged him but he denied it of course, and so I started trying to trap him and find out what was going on. It was horrible, horrible, horrible. This went on for several months and I got increasingly stressed. My British colleagues were saying, "You need to go home and take a break," and my Rwandan lady friends were saying, "It's OK. Our men do this all the time. He'll come back. Just wait and be patient." I just didn't know what to do but then he decided to move out and although it was horrible, it did ease the pressure a little bit. We asked some friends from the church in Kigali to come and talk things through with us and we had one meeting with them. There was also a lot of unhappiness at that time because Anatolie's six-year old daughter had just died of malaria.

That sounds like a very difficult time. How did you get through it?

I was crying a lot and not coping at work so at the end of March 1994 I decided to have a two-week holiday in Kenya with my sister, Sue. She flew out from Scotland to join me but just a few days after we reached Mombasa we got the news that the Rwandan genocide had started. The President had been killed and everything was in utter chaos. We didn't have access to a phone and so we were completely out of touch.

We needed to get to Nairobi but when we tried to do that we found that all the trains had been cancelled because of a derailment. Eventually, we managed to get a lift but the drive took a whole day and night and Sue was very ill with food poisoning. She wouldn't drink because we were driving through game parks where you couldn't get out of the car to go to the loo. It was terrible. When we got to the Tearfund guest house in Nairobi we found loads of faxes spilling on to the floor. They were all telling me to contact my manager and saying that I must not under any circumstances attempt to go back to Kigali.

My first reaction was that I wanted to go back because Charles was there and my work was there. But I was told that the airport was under guard and I wouldn't be able to go anywhere because there was no public transport. So I waited in Nairobi and stayed glued to my short-wave radio. It was extremely difficult to find out what was going on but then I met up with some expat colleagues. They had tried to stay but had eventually been forced to flee, and they gave me the terrible news that Anatolie and her husband had been killed. Their three-year old daughter had also been attacked but had survived. Once I knew that I really couldn't go back, there was no point in staying in Nairobi so my sister and I flew back to the UK. My manager at Tearfund had very kindly vacated her flat in London for me to stay in, and Sue went up to Scotland.

How did you fill your time?

I found it very hard to face anyone. Friends wanted to visit but I couldn't cope. All I was doing was watching the news on TV, listening to the radio and buying newspapers. I'd see the rows of bodies and think, "Do I recognise any of the shoes? Do I know anyone there?" It was just awful. The world was in shock about what had happened and when the media found out I had first-hand experience of Rwanda I did lots of TV and newspaper interviews. When I moved back up to Scotland I also did a lot of Tearfund talks in schools and churches—I always asked people to pray for Charles and for Rwanda. And of course I had all this ambivalent stuff going on because my marriage had been in a mess. But I had to park those thoughts and think, "Never mind about all of that—the most important thing is that he's found alive." So everything was all over the place.

By July, the country was still in utter turmoil but the genocide had pretty much finished so I started saying to Tearfund that I wanted to go back. I'd heard rumours about what might have happened to Charles and I needed to know for certain. At first they said that it was too dangerous and I was too broken, but eventually they agreed and so in September I went back with Tearfund's head of HR. I was so grateful for her support.

What did you find when you got there?

One of the first people I contacted was my sister-in-law. Her seven children had all fled during the genocide and had survived by hiding in neighbours' homes. We met up and then we went to a diocesan guesthouse in the south of the country. I'd heard reports that Charles fled there because he had a friend who worked on the border post. He'd been hoping to get out of the country but it turned out that his friend had already fled, so it was too late. We met with the Bishop and he showed us the room where Charles had stayed. Then he told us that a car had come with some soldiers in it. They'd said they were looking for Tutsis and had taken Charles away. That was the last the Bishop had seen of him.

I remember coming away from the meeting and my sister-in-law saying, "That man has my brother's blood on his hands." We both felt that if the Bishop had hidden Charles then he would still be alive. I was very angry and then I discovered that the Bishop's wife was a Tutsi and they already had several of her family hidden in the house. If he'd taken other people then everyone would have been at risk. So that put a different perspective on it for me. And it also meant that I had to face the fact that Charles was dead. I'd kept thinking, "Maybe we'll find him. Maybe I'll see him in the street." But my sister-in-law said, "No. This is a small country. If he were still alive somewhere, I'd have heard about it by now." That was the first time that I thought, "Gosh. He is dead. I'm a widow."

It was also when I had to accept that God hadn't answered my prayers, and that was difficult because I'd prayed madly. At all those talks I'd given, I'd asked people to pray for Charles to be kept safe, and I'd thought, "When he comes back I'll contact all these people and we'll show that God really does answer prayers." I was clinging on to my faith and thinking, "It's alright—God knows what he's doing—Charles is in a better place—onwards and upwards and let's be strong—keep trusting God—and all that sort of thing." I really didn't allow myself to acknowledge the horror of it.

What were you doing at that stage?

Towards the end of that year I decided to write a book. I'd noticed that whenever I said anything about living in Rwanda, there was a kind of shock horror reaction—*That country is just full of savages who are killing each other.* And I'd think, "*What*? That place was my home with my friends and family, and good people. I don't want people to just think it's a terrible place." And so I decided to show that through telling my own story.

I was still quite unsettled after that and thought I might go back to Rwanda again but not in a healthcare role—perhaps teaching in a local Bible college. So I went and studied theology for a couple of years at All Nations Christian College in Hertfordshire and then the staff asked if I would stay on and teach pastoral studies. I did that and trained as a pastoral counsellor but eventually the traumas started to catch up with me. I wasn't looking after myself properly and felt burned out. I was also finding church difficult. I'd go to services and keep thinking, "How can you praise God? Where *is* God, anyway?" I'd leave feeling worse than when I went in so I handed in my notice at the college and stopped going to church altogether. I thought I'd probably come back to it at some point but I just needed to give it up for a bit.

Over the next few years God was still there but I couldn't

do the being positive stuff, and the nice neat answers and the 'Don't worry, everything will work out and God's in control...' I'd think, "How can you say that? That's not *my* experience." And I didn't have anyone I could talk to about it. All my friends were ardently involved in the Church and I felt very out of it. During that time I did some admin work at a further education college, and all sorts of other bits and pieces.

Then my mother wasn't well so I went back up to Scotland to help look after her. And that was the point at which I started going back to church.

Did you find out what happened to Charles?

About ten years after the genocide I was approached by a media company. They said they'd take me out to Rwanda and try to help me find out what had happened to him. And when they asked if I could forgive his killers, I said, "I don't know. I've thought a lot about forgiveness. I've talked about it and I've written about it but blimey—if I had to face somebody could I actually forgive?" I wasn't sure whether I wanted to put myself through all of that but in the end I said I would and we spent a month in Rwanda.

We went back to see the Bishop and we met people who were in prison on crimes of genocide including a man who'd been part of the group that killed Anatolie. I also met Anatolie's little daughter. We didn't find out who was responsible for Charles's death and I found that very traumatic as all these difficult issues had been raised again but without any resolution. When I came back to the UK, I wrote a second book about that experience.

I decided to ask Fergal Keane if he would write a

commendation for the book as he'd been one of the BBC correspondents in Rwanda during the genocide and I'd been very impressed by the way he reported on it. I was thrilled when he agreed to write something and then some time later I got a phone call out of the blue from someone at the BBC. They were planning to make a programme with Fergal, in Northern Ireland and to bring people from different sides of the conflict together with a panel of mediators. I was stunned when they asked me to be on the panel with Archbishop Desmond Tutu and the Harvard academic Donna Hicks who has done reconciliation work in war zones around the world. The BBC team said they wanted someone with personal experience. My first reaction was, "Good grief, I need to think about this." I phoned my brother and Gareth to ask what I should do, and they both said, "Get on with it!" So the upshot was that I spent ten days in Northern Ireland with Desmond Tutu, Donna Hicks, Fergal Keane, and a film crew making a series called *Facing the Truth.*

That must have been difficult...

It was incredibly moving and such a privilege to sit there and hear people tell their stories. There was one woman I remember whose husband had been killed and she was really struggling with the situation. I talked to her during a break in the filming and she said, "I hated sitting there looking at this man who killed my husband, but I kept looking at you and thinking that Lesley has done this and she's still together so if she can do it, I can do it." Making that series was an extraordinary experience. The team all worked brilliantly together and we've kept in touch and had reunions. Then four years ago, I asked Desmond Tutu if he would preach at my ordination. He agreed and it was the most incredibly precious thing. That's a long answer to your original question, but it's how I got to where I am now. I've cared for people's physical health as a nurse—I've cared for their emotional health as a counsellor—I've worked in reconciliation and tried to bring communities together—but there was always something missing and that led me to become ordained. I don't think that there can be wholeness without God.

What does forgiveness mean to you now?

I hate it when people say *forgive and forget* because when something major has happened, you can't—it stays with you. It's important to acknowledge that it was awful and that you were very angry. I haven't always done that but now I can see that until you let go of the bitterness and anger, you can't move on. There was a chap I met in a Rwandan prison when I was making the TV documentary. His attitude was horrible. I was sure that he knew more than he was prepared to say and that he may have had something to do with Charles's death. But instead of saying what he knew, he played a kind of power game with me. Every time I thought about it, I felt churned up—I was so angry with him. Then eventually, I got to a point where I knew I must put it behind me and stop this man having power over me. And part of that letting go, was thinking about his circumstances and wondering what led him to do those things. It seemed like he was in a pretty sad situation and so I prayed that he would not be stuck in his bitterness and anger. We're all human and I've got some things wrong in my own life, so who am I to hold resentments towards anyone whether it's about big things or everyday situations? Instead I want to wish for them to have life in all its fullness. But of course, that's easier said than done. The past has caught up with me afresh recently and now twenty-five years on I'm seeing a psychotherapist and letting go of some of it. There's a lot of sadness and tears but I'm finding it extremely helpful.

The traumas were awful things that I would never wish on anyone, and yet incomprehensibly out of them, amazing things have happened. I can sit alongside people who are bereaved or hurting or going through unspeakable traumas. They might be railing at God and I can be with them, and share some of my story if that's appropriate. Some of them might say, “You understand.” I feel very passionately about God bringing beauty out of brokenness. In fact, I see that as central to my faith. When Jesus’s body was broken and he died, everyone thought that was the end but it wasn’t. Each week we re-enact this when we take, break and share bread in Church at the Eucharist—new life out of death, beauty out of brokenness. Things going wrong aren't a barrier to fullness and in fact it's often through brokenness that we discover real depths and riches.

I'm a bit fixated on that and that's how my second book, *With What Remains,* got its name. I came across a story of the violinist Itzhak Perlman. He had polio as a child and walks with crutches and yet despite this severe disability he has risen to the top of his profession. In the film *Schindler's List* there's this beautiful, haunting violin solo all the way through, and that's him. Anyway, the story goes that he was in the middle of a concert when one of his strings broke and somehow he managed to keep going. He played fantastically and after the rapturous applause, a woman went up to him and said “How on earth did you do that?" His answer was "Madam, my job is to make music with what remains." That made me think about the people of Rwanda. They're making music with what remains and that's what I want to do with my life, too.

May 2018

Nicholas

"I started to dream about coming back to Rwanda—I wanted to be part of the process of healing our nation"

When Lesley said that she was passing me on to her friend in Rwanda I was a bit thrown. How would I do the interview? Could a video call ever be as satisfactory as meeting face-to-face? This was, remember, before Covid made Zoom calls a normal way to interact. I'd already considered and dismissed the idea of limiting the interviewees to women and now here was a new question. Should I have limited it to interviewees in the UK where I could meet face-to-face? But of course, it made perfect sense that Lesley would choose someone from the country that has played such an important part in her life. And I didn't have to think very long before realising that whilst this is a new departure, it is an exciting development.

Lesley tells me that Nicholas is the most humble man she knows. She adds some background information,"Nicholas is a Hutu and Elsie his wife is a Tutsi. She was a bridesmaid at my wedding and we've been friends for years. Together Nicholas and Elsie have done some phenomenal reconciliation work with widows from both sides of the genocide. They've been through much worse things than me and have still managed to pick up the pieces, trust in God, and move on in their lives. They are lovely, lovely people and I am so in awe of them."

I contact Nicholas by email and he says he's happy to do a video call. We fix a date but on the day we are due to speak, he emails to say that he has had to make an emergency trip up country and so he's not available. Can we reschedule for a week ahead? I have no idea what an emergency trip up country could mean in Rwanda but it's a reminder that his life is very different from mine and I look forward to learning more about it.

When we get to speak my fears are allayed and the technology works perfectly. Nicholas is in Kigali, the capital of Rwanda, and I can hear the busy sounds of early evening traffic in the background. He's open and friendly but gets straight to the point—"When you talk to any Rwandan, the genocide is a reference point. For us, when we narrate our story, we'll tell you if something happened before the genocide, or after. It's like Before Christ or After Christ."

What was your early life like, Nicholas?

I grew up in a village in a very remote area of Rwanda. My parents were subsistence farmers with nine children and we all had to work very hard and help to get food on the table. We were poor but we lived happily together, and when we had food to eat we were very happy. Everything that we ate came from our own farm. We had cows and we grew beans, sweet potatoes, bananas and cassava. We fetched water from the river and a spring, and washed ourselves in a nearby stream—that's the kind of life that we had.

My family was Christian and from a young age our parents would take us to church. They also paid for us all to go to primary school. But then I passed the National Exam to go to secondary school and that was a huge problem for my parents. They didn't know how to pay for my fees. Then my brother who was a tailor said, "OK I will support you. Let him go." My family went through hardship and made sacrifices for me.

What happened after you left school?

After school I went to university and in 1989 I graduated as an agricultural engineer. By then I'd already known Elsie for five years and we were engaged. I got a job and we started to plan our wedding. It was 1991 when we were married and just like any other young couple, we had many dreams. I was working on an agricultural project funded by the World Bank and we were planning to build our own house. But then, when our first son, Jonathan, was four months old, the genocide started and we had to flee.

At that time the population of Rwanda was around seven million, and about a seventh of the population was killed over the space of a hundred days. More than 600,000 women and children were widowed and orphaned, and several million people fled to other countries as refugees. What happened to us in Rwanda was on an unimaginable scale.

There were miracles, though, and one was that we survived the genocide. It started on April 6th and it wasn't until 27th May that we managed to cross the border into Congo. There was so much killing during that time and I feel that God helped us in many different ways, to escape. When we crossed over the border, Elsie and I looked back and said that we would never come back to Rwanda. I felt I didn't want to see this country again. This country that was killing its own people. I didn't even want to be called a Rwandan—I felt so ashamed of what our people had done. My wife had lost most of her people—her Dad, her brothers, her sisters and more. In Africa, we don't just talk about the nuclear family of *Mum and Dad and children*, we include all the aunties and uncles and cousins. She lost over 120 people that were close relatives. They were a part of who she is. Elsie and I both survived—we did not have physical scars like many survivors do but like many others we were suffering inside. And sometimes you don't know what has happened to you, when it's all been so sudden. For a person to be able to recover—well, it takes miracles. It's not a given.

How did you cope with the trauma?

We had survived the genocide and were outside Rwanda but what had happened in Rwanda was still being carried around in our hearts. And to make matters more complicated, Elsie and I had different interpretations of what happened. We were a young couple who had no experience of handling such things.

One of the hardest things was that I am from a historically Hutu background and Elsie is from a Tutsi background. To be correct they aren't really different ethnic groups at all—the division only came about because Belgian colonists wrongly classified the population when they produced the first written history of Rwanda. But that knowledge is all with the benefit of hindsight and we grew up with this division. My wife's group had suffered thirty years of persecutions and killings that were hardly acknowledged. Then when the genocide happened and we survived, it was like an emotional volcano erupting for her. We hurt each other and we both said things we should not have said. It has been a journey with a lot of pain.

In my family background, and especially with it being a Christian upbringing, there was no issue about ethnic divisions. I was aware of the differences but there was no problem when Elsie and I decided to get married. Even though the war had started by that time, we loved one another and then even throughout the genocide we had no problems with difference. I tried to protect her and the fact that we got out of the country and she was physically unharmed was a miracle. But when we went across the border, that was when we started to feel all of the emotions and to think about all of the history. Neither of us was prepared for that. She saw me as one of those who killed—I didn't understand why she could not see that I wasn't one of them.

That must have been enormously difficult...

A few months after the genocide ended, Lesley came back to try and discover what had happened to her husband, and she found us in Kenya. She decided to start a trust fund in her husband's Charles's name, to help Rwandans recover from the trauma of the genocide, and it was that trust fund that made it possible for Elsie, our son and me to go and live in Edinburgh. I did a masters degree and a PhD there. We spent over six years in Scotland and experienced so much love and help from people we had never met but who contributed money for this family who had fled from Rwanda. They put us into a semi-detached house in a very good neighbourhood close to the University of Edinburgh and provided every single thing we needed for over six years while we were in Scotland. They provided a space where we could begin to process what had happened to us—we look back at all the love we received and say, "Why us?"

It was very hard but the turning point for us came in 1996. In December of that year I went to a meeting in Detmold in Germany. Christians from churches in Rwanda and elsewhere came together to think about how we'd arrived at these problems, and how we could rebuild Rwandan society. And it was during this time that I realised why someone with a Tutsi background like Elsie, would identify me, with my Hutu background, with those who had killed during the genocide. That was a huge realisation—a weight of responsibility which I had been denying for over two years.

I never killed anyone and had in fact been trying to save lives but any of my contemporaries could see me as one of *them*. And that was when I felt the need to apologise to people who had suffered in the genocide and to identify with their pain. I knew all about it because my wife had gone through it and I knew exactly what she was feeling. During the meeting, the participants (including me) wrote what came to be known as the Confession of Detmold. It was a really new and unique experience that all the different groups—the Hutus, the Tutsis and the Westerners—were able to repent and ask for forgiveness. At the end of that experience I had a beautiful vision of a new nation, a new country and a new society reconciled to itself. And that was when I said to Elsie, “Forgive me, forgive my attitude and my lack of compassion.” That was a turning point in the problems between us and we came to an understanding. It was so powerful. At that stage I had just finished my masters degree and was starting on my PhD.

After that, I started to dream about coming back to Rwanda. I wanted to be part of the process of healing our nation and to be one of the people who could help others. I presented my dissertation at the end of 2000 and in July 2001 we returned to Rwanda.

How did it feel to arrive back in Rwanda?

I had mixed emotions. When we went to Edinburgh there were just three of us but we had two other children while we were there and so we were now a family of five. As we flew away over Edinburgh I felt a huge burden of responsibility. I was taking my entire family away from this place of safety. But we also felt that the six years we had spent in Scotland were a huge privilege. We received so much and now we were keen to give back in knowledge, skills, hard work, and love.

We were ready to do something transformational with our lives but I cannot say we were very encouraged by the first few weeks when we got back to Kigali. Before 1994 my wife and I had so many friends there and we were always welcoming people and being welcomed. But this time, after we arrived, only one family came to see us, and apart from that there was just Elsie and me and the kids. When the kids were in bed, I remember Elsie asking, "Are we going to spend more than a year without anyone coming to visit us?" It felt like we were starting a long, lonely journey but then one evening a family came to visit, and then another one came and then more. That felt like a miracle. It was not an easy time but we had great determination and faith that it was the right thing to do.

What is your life like at the moment?

Most of my time now I'm managing a social agri-business which I started thirteen years ago. Poverty creates great challenges in itself but when you add in our recent history—the genocide, the war, people in refugee camps—it becomes an even bigger problem for the poor. The business is called Ikirezi Natural Products and our vision is to reach out to very poor rural people, particularly widows, orphans and women, and to offer them the chance to earn an income. Many other models give people handouts but we work differently. We say to the poor, "We trust that you have what it takes to move from what you have and where you are, to another level. And we'll create a conducive environment to help you do that." Ikirezi provides them with well-paid farming jobs. The hope is that over time this helps people to regain their dignity and to feel valued.

You know, poverty is like leprosy—one feels disempowered and abandoned. But once you provide decent jobs you see the lives of poor people really starting to improve. With a better livelihood their social status improves and their health improves, too. We also bring a kind of holistic healing into their lives by providing a safe environment where they can talk through what has happened to them and their families.

Part of our work is to try and transform people's mindsets. Subsistence farmers eat what they grow and do not normally plan ahead. That's how they have to be—there is no way to look ahead when you cannot even see where you are putting your feet right now. Our crops are different. We are teaching farmers to grow cash crops. They are for export. We grow aromatic plants that are used to make essential oils such as geranium, lemon grass, patchouli, rosemary, and lavandin. We export the oils to the US, UK and South Africa. We deal with the whole value chain from the growing and processing to the exporting. We've also started manufacturing some end-products with the oils. All of that helps us to provide more jobs and to raise more revenue from what we grow. My team and I were not familiar with essential oils when we started so we've all learned together with the farmers and that has been a tremendous journey.

One of the heartbreaking realities of producing raw materials in Africa for export to the West, is that everyone involved in the value chain wants to get a bigger piece of the cake. So there might be thirty percent profit margin for the processor, twenty percent for the transporter, thirty percent for the trader and manufacturer and even some more for the retailer. And in the effort to produce affordable products, it's the people at the bottom of the value chain who get squeezed the most. The farmers get paid less and less whereas others in the value chain get a fair share of the profit margin. We feel that these people who are working so hard deserve to be paid better and to be treated well. I can tell you that one day of minimum wage in the UK could be more than a month's salary for a farmer here. So we have been trying to see how we can make a business that helps the poor to earn a decent wage.

We have a way of incentivising people to work hard and make progress. They might start as part of a team of twenty at the beginning and get paid, say, the equivalent of $1 a day. We assess how things are going every month, and use set criteria. If the weeding is done well and the crop is well tended, for example, then we give the workers a raise to maybe $1.20 a day. If they continue to work well then it could go up to $1.50. That's a real accomplishment and means they have learned the techniques and are trusted to work well. It's a way of helping them to grow and helping us to grow, by competing within themselves.

Can you tell me about some people that you've helped?

We've been so happy and surprised to see people surmount problems and transform themselves. There are so many stories but I want to tell you about one young man. Ten years ago he was living in rural poverty with his brothers and his widowed mother. His father died and they didn't have a proper home. They didn't even have enough land to grow their own food. They were really hungry and desperate. So this young man joined Ikirezi and he worked very hard. After three or four years of paid farming work he was able to earn enough money to buy a piece of land and to build his own house. This house is one of the best in his neighbourhood. He got married and now has three kids. He's a confident young man who has been able to provide for his family. Only about seventeen percent of the rural population in Rwanda has electricity and he's been able to put in solar power electricity in his house. That means they now have light. He's one of our best farmers and I often call on him to train others. He has worked hard and is good at what he does. His life has changed.

Another story I can tell you is about a widow who had no source of income. Now that she works with us, she has been able to build herself a house, send her kids to school, and is even paying for one of them to go to university. It's a totally different situation from ten years ago when she joined the scheme. People are able to do a lot with very little money.

Looking back how do you feel about what has happened to you?

For Elsie and me, our views were shaped by our Christian faith prior to the genocide—despite all the propaganda to hate *the other* we were taught that we are all created by God and that our differences complement one another. That Christian faith has sustained us through all the troubles. During the genocide we prayed to God to help us—I cannot answer why others were killed and not us. But I know that we saw the providence of God's hand.

As I said earlier I felt a great sense of responsibility when I brought my family back to Rwanda. It was like a compulsion, a calling. I felt I was being told, "That's why you were born Rwandan—to play a role in a time such as this. You have to spend your life there." It was very hard at the time but I remember saying, "OK if we go back and even one life is transformed, then it will be worth it."

Now that the children have grown up, I can say that we've had thousands of challenges but none of us has ever regretted coming back. The overwhelming feeling is that we are in the right place and doing what we are meant to be doing. That gives us tremendous encouragement.

July 2018

Becca

"There are a lot of myths about why women are on the streets"

With Nicholas's handover the chain turns westwards and travels over seven thousand miles across the Atlantic Ocean to the United States. Like Nicholas, Becca runs a social enterprise but hers serves a very different client group. It's based in Nashville where Becca is also an Episcopal minister. Nicholas speaks very warmly of her. They've been friends for ten years and he says, "When you get time to talk to Becca, you will quickly understand why she is so inspiring."

Becca responds positively to my email and says that she's happy to help. Then as she travels a lot and has a complicated schedule she passes me to her assistant so that we can liaise on arrangements. We fix a date for a phone call a few weeks ahead and I get a sense that Becca's time is much in demand. Once again I'm very grateful that all of these interesting people have believed in the project, and given me time.

When Becca and I get to speak it's the week before Christmas. She tells me about the traumas in her own early life and how they led her to set up Thistle Farms—a community of women survivors of trafficking, addiction and prostitution. There are now about fifty affiliated communities in the United States as well as global partners around the world. Their Magdalene recovery program has helped hundreds of women to break harmful cycles and rebuild their lives. As well as writing nine books about the transformational power of love, Becca has been named 'Humanitarian of the Year' by the Small Business Council of America, a 'CNN Hero', and a White House 'Champion of Change'.

What are the main things in your life right now, Becca?

It's two decades since I became the founder and president of Thistle Farms and right now you've caught me in a space where I am so grateful. I've raised three beautiful boys with my husband of thirty years, and the Thistle Farms community is supporting more than 1,800 survivors. There's a lot of love, and it's harvest time—but it didn't start that way.

How did Thistle Farms come about?

I guess that it came out of moving from brokenness in my own life into understanding and compassion. The story began in 1968 when my Mom and Dad moved from New York to Nashville. He was an Episcopal priest and not long after the move he was killed by a drunk driver. That left my Mom with five little kids and she raised us by herself. She was amazing. But unfortunately for me, the man that helped run the church after my father's death, began sexually abusing me—it started when I was five and went on for years. There was plenty of stuff that got messed up in my life but I think even then I knew I didn't want that fear and loneliness to be my story. I always had a really loving family and there were some great people in the community that helped me with education and forgave me a lot.

Because of what happened to me, I always had a heart for these women that were on the streets and had gone through some similar stuff. So after I got ordained I started thinking about how to help. That's how Thistle Farms came about. I wanted to create a beautiful home and a free space where women could stay for a couple of years and find the healing they need. The idea we try to hold is that we're a loving community. Love is the most powerful force for change in our lives. And we also believe in a housing-first model—in being able to say, "Here's your key. You live here."

The first five women moved into the house in 1997. They came from the streets and from prison, and within a few months I knew that this was going to change my life. I'd longed to believe that it's possible to heal from some of the worst and oldest and deepest scars that humanity has to offer, and suddenly I could witness it. It was a huge part of my own healing journey, too. That, and going to Divinity School at Vanderbilt University where I met my husband. He's a country singer-songwriter and helped to start the Thistle Farms community. He's written a lot about this stuff and he's done really well.

Tell me about the impact of Thistle Farms...

When women come to Thistle Farms they're basically committing the next two years of their life to finding their way back home. They spend the first six months working on their body and mind. So it could mean that they need to do some work on addiction, on post-traumatic stress, getting healthcare, getting teeth, getting restitution with their children through the courts—it could be any number of things.

After that, they get to come to work. Many of the women we serve are first raped between the ages of seven and eleven, and then they hit the streets between fourteen and sixteen years old. So they don't have any work experience other than surviving on the streets and going to prison. We try to offer a trauma-informed place where they can start working and earning money. At Thistle Farms we make and sell things like candles, bath products, and home goods. They're all really luxurious and we use essential oils that Nicholas produces in Rwanda. Then the second year in the community is all about preparing the women to live on their own. We have a plan that matches any savings they make, we have life skills classes, they can go to college—and if they want to stay on at Thistle Farms they can train to take on more of a management position. There are all kinds of options and they mean that the women never have to go back to the streets—they never have to go to prison again. They can get a car, a place to live, they can have their own bank account, and make decisions about what they wear and how they spend their time. These things make a radical difference.

I saw some of that this morning. We have this tradition of beginning every day at work by sitting in a circle. Someone does a reading and people make reflections. Today, many of the women were talking about this being their *First Christmas*. It's the first time they've bought presents for their children, or the first time they've got to see their parents, or had a Christmas tree, or a Christmas present. The first time *ever*.

One woman I can tell you about is Ty. Her experience of sexual assault started with her stepfather when she was in middle school. She quickly ended up on the streets and the way she tells her story is that when other girls were thinking about what dress to get for their prom, she was trying to figure out which cars to get in and out of. She was running drugs too, for her pimp and was involved in a sting. She came to our program from prison and was doing really well. But she still had one charge pending and about a year after she started with us she got sentenced to fourteen more years. That was a really sad, hard day. It took a lot of advocacy and work but she came back to our community after three years and was completely free of addiction. She got married and had a child with her husband. These days she directs the manufacturing at Thistle Farms. When the women come in she trains them to make these beautiful lavish products—candles and bath salts. She's a joy and is completely fearless.

Another woman is Sheila. Her trafficking journey began when she was five years old. Her mother sold her all over the USA, and then she ended up prostituting herself. About fifteen years ago she came to us and decided that she really needed to go back to school. She got a degree in social work and twelve years ago she married the love of her life in my living room. They've had two children and Nicholas Kristof of the *New York Times* wrote an article about her called *From the Streets to the 'World's Best Mom'*. Now she's the director of our whole national network. Recently she and I went to Mexico to visit a small group of women who run their own justice enterprise. When they talked about what they needed to get started it was Sheila who made the first donation. Even though she's done really well, she knows how hard the struggle is. She's lived it and these days she lives out her gratitude.

What are the biggest challenges?

About 80% of the women that come into the program stick with it, but of course this means that 20% don't. As you can imagine, we've had a lot of hard, horrible stories along the way. Sometimes women go back into a dangerous relationship and then pretty soon they head back to the streets. Some are murdered or end up in jail. Relapse is our biggest challenge. Another is keeping the core staff together. It's exhausting when you put a lot of time and energy into someone and then they quit, and you have to start over again.

The third challenge is money. We're rich now because it's Christmas but in the summer, money can be really tight.

How do you fund Thistle Farms?

We began selling our products in 2001 and that's been a good source of income. But we've never had government or state funding for our programs so in the beginning all the money came from individual donations. The idea was to find people who wanted to hope with us, and invest and see a beautiful return on that investment. We would say, "Offering a woman a place at Thistle Farms will cost us $22,000 a year and that's a quarter of what it costs to keep her in prison. And if she comes to us, she'll never have to go back to prison again."

There are a lot of myths about why women are on the streets. And we tell people that none of them got there by themselves. It took a community and broken systems to do that, and it takes a community to respond and welcome the women home. All the research shows that if you want a really good investment in a community then you should invest in the women—it changes everything. You rape a woman and you kill a village but if you heal a woman you heal a whole village. You're not just helping that woman, you're influencing their whole network and helping to stop damage passing down the generations. Some of the women in our community say to us, "Here's my cousin, here's my daughter, here's my sister, and they want what I have." There's always a waiting list.

How do you feel about the men that perpetrate these crimes on women?

We call them *johns* in the US—men who are arrested for solicitation. And here we have a school for them with many men coming through our community for a day. They learn to humanise women and hear about their backstories. What we've learned over the years is that a lot of men have backstories too. If you're going to have compassion then you need to have compassion for everybody. That doesn't mean that you don't hold people accountable, and it doesn't mean that you sweep justice under the rug, but it means that you can hear stories and have compassion, and believe that there's a path out. So, for example, in our circle time we often have men who've been sex addicts. It's become part of the healing process for everyone. You think you're gonna hate all the johns. But you don't.

How do you feel you've changed through working with women?

I've changed in a bunch of ways. When I started out I probably believed more things than I believe now. But what I'm left believing, I believe with my whole heart. I believe in love. That's the biggest change in me. I don't have a lot of dogmatic beliefs left, but I am dogged about how I love people and how I practise that in a daily way. It needs to be practical. I think it's about being there for good times and bad times, and a lot of times it means we have to suspend judgement—trying to actively hear the person and to maybe ask a nice question, rather than thinking about what's wrong with them. We are so quick to judge.

We need to love ourselves too. I'm pretty disciplined about doing yoga and taking care of my body, and I use the oils that Nicholas makes. By loving each other and ourselves we can do amazing healing work. We can do it with dignity and compassion, and we can do it with gratitude.

This chain series reminds us that our stories connect us all. Like with Nicholas. We got to know each other through our work but now our sons are friends and our family stories are connected. People all have so much in common and the lines that divide us are infinitesimal. The difference between a priest and a prostitute is nothing.

What does gratitude mean to you, Becca?

I think that gratitude is the closest I come to faith. There's been horrible stuff but there are always stories of transformation and wholeness that come through, and a sense of there being so much to be grateful for. And when I can stay in that space of gratitude then it really does connect me to God.

What's next for you?

The focus this coming year is on strengthening our global partnerships. We want to move more women out of poverty and that means that we have to expand our markets, get more funding and have really good strategic plans. So this year I'm headed all over. In January I'm going to Rwanda to help Nicholas start a rabbit farm. That will produce liquid fertiliser for his plants and we're going to talk about ways to increase product opportunities and local markets for his oils. Our partnership continues to grow. Then I'll be going to

Belize, Mexico and Ecuador. We're also working hard on a project that provides income and skills to Syrian women at a refugee camp in Greece. They weave welcome doormats from the life vests and blankets that they received when they landed. It's going so well that we've had to establish a not-for-profit enterprise in the UK to sell the mats. It's called *Love Welcomes* and is our newest partnership.

I also want to write another book. This time about how I've experienced prayer in so many different ways around the world, and in circles of women—singing, drumming, telling stories. It's not just about people reciting words. And just this morning I found out that we've reached the four million dollars mark for Thistle Farm sales this year. Isn't that amazing? I'm so lucky to be a part of it. I can share some of the story, and hold the history—and love the women. It's the best.

December 2018

Mike

"This community that had put up with police brutality and oppression over and over and over again, came out—I never met Mike Brown but he changed my life"

After Nashville the next stop is Pasadena in California where I'm going to be talking to another Episcopal priest. Becca describes Mike as her "true friend."

There's a mix-up with emails so when I contact Mike it's the first he knows about the project but he is immediately enthusiastic. "WOW," he says. "What an amazing project. Absolutely *I will do this." He also expresses amazement that Becca has nominated him and says that if he had to name someone who had inspired* him *then she would be the first person that came to mind. I see evidence of this in his standard e-mail template. After the sign-off is a quote from Becca's book Find Your Way Home—"We love the women still walking the streets, the people who have turned away from us, and the people we thought we could not love. This is the kind of radical love that can change the world."*

Becca's assistant had warned me that Mike might take a while to respond as he's very busy but he tells me that Friday mornings are fine as that's his day off. We agree to have a video call at 10am PST which is 6pm GMT, the time difference now an implicit reminder that the person holding the other end of the chain is a long way from where I started.

When we talk, Mike is relaxed and genial. He explains that community is at the heart of his philosophy and then gives a vivid description of what happened when he was involved in a series of remarkable events. They made headlines globally and changed America forever. Not for the first time in this project I feel awe at talking to someone who can give a personal account of world-changing events.

How did you get to know Becca?

It goes back to the late 1990s when I was young and newly ordained. A group of us discovered that out of 10,000 priests in the Episcopal Church, fewer than 300 were aged under 35. So we decided to put on a conference for everyone in that group. It was my job to vet the workshop proposals and one came in from this priest in Nashville called Becca. I read her letter, and a newspaper article she'd included about Magdalene, the community she'd just started for women survivors of prostitution, violence and drug abuse. And I thought, "It sounds almost too good to be true—and I'm going to that workshop." So I did and that's where we first met.

At that time, my job included campus ministry and I asked Becca if I could take some of the students down to Nashville so they could spend time with the women and share ideas and just be together. When I got there I realised it was everything that Becca had said it was—and more. It's the heart of priesthood and the heart of Christian community and ever since then it's been my model. When I was Dean of Christ Church Cathedral in St. Louis we gathered a group of people together so that St. Louis could start our own Magdalene community. It's called *Bravely*. Like the Nashville model, it's a two-year residential community operating on the same principles. For their social enterprise, the women make things like T-shirts and tote bags. People from the wider community are involved, not just the church congregation, and we opened the first house about four years ago. I'm in Pasadena now and every year I bring Becca and some of the Nashville women out here to talk and to remind us about the spiritual principles of Magdalene.

What led you to become a priest, Mike?

I was raised in a split-faith household and both of my parents were astronomers. My father was Church of England as he grew up in Britain, and my Mom belongs to a church called Self-Realisation Fellowship (SRF) which combines Eastern and Western beliefs. So I grew up with the idea that spirituality is central to life and it's about finding your own right path. And that having the right path for you doesn't mean that everyone else is wrong. SRF has been wonderful for my Mom and I tried it for a while but then when I was about thirteen, I went to an Episcopal summer camp. What I found was people being honest about who they were, and living with love and integrity in a community. And I thought, "If this is what Jesus is about, then I'm *in*." SRF was great but as the name says, it's mostly about how you progress to the higher self and I've always been much more interested in community. I remember one particular night at the camp when we were all gathered together and there was this girl called Lisa who was about a year older than me. She stepped up and said, "I want to share this poem that I wrote." I have no memory of the poem itself but I know that I thought, "Wow, this is a place where it's safe enough to be *that* vulnerable—to *really* be yourself."

It had crossed my mind when I was at school, that I might be a priest but only in the same way that I thought I might be a baseball player, or maybe run for political office or something like that. In fact, what I did after school was to go to the University of Missouri and do a degree in journalism. I love writing and I'm a huge sports fan so I thought I'd like to be a sports writer. But I realised pretty quick that I wasn't finding the depth of meaning that I wanted. At the time I was part of a church where we had a phenomenal rector called Jim Fallis. He followed the village priest model so his congregation was not just the people who came to church on Sunday, it was everyone else in the area, too. He created communities of love wherever he went and I knew that was where I could find the deepest joy and meaning. After a while, people there started saying to me, "You need to think about being a priest," and it just felt right. So I went off to seminary and got ordained.

What was it like when you went out into the world as a priest?

My first job was in St. Louis and I spent part of my time on the university campus gathering together a community of college students. The wonderful thing about that community was that they were able to be together, and love each other and be real with each other. And when there was conflict they really struggled to try and solve it. Those students wouldn't let me put on priest airs with them or be anything less than honest, and even though I've been a priest for over twenty years I know I'm at my best when I function as I did when I was a college chaplain. That absolutely shaped me.

We had so many amazing students—and something that was hugely life-changing for me involved one of our students named Julia McNeely. She was one of those people that held the community together like glue. She was planning to go to Tanzania to start a ministry for street kids when she graduated from college. Then one day when she was driving home for Christmas she hydroplaned on a rainy road. Another car hit her and she was killed instantly. After all these years I still can't talk about Julia without crying and our community had to do some deep healing work. It left me with the constant reminder that things can end really quickly. And to keep asking myself, "How am I loving right now?"

What are the most important things that you can do as a priest?

There are two pieces of scripture that guide my life and remind me how I want to be. The first is when God is talking to Moses and says, "I have heard the cry of my people in their oppression and I will come down and deliver them." That's God saying, "It's not enough to stay above everything. I'm getting down in the mud with the pain of humanity."

The second is the story of Jesus and the blind beggar Bartimaeus, from the Gospel of St. Mark. It's when Jesus is on the way to Jerusalem with his disciples. He's got places to go and people to see and then they pass this blind beggar crying out by the side of the road. The disciples tell the beggar to shut up but Jesus stops and asks, "What would you have me do for you?" That's what a loving community looks like—an awareness of how everyone's life is, and having people on the margins take center place in the community and set the agenda.

How do you put those principles into practice?

There are many ways but one particular life-changing event happened in 2014. At that time I was Dean of Christ Church Cathedral right in the heart of downtown St. Louis. Something you need to understand is that St. Louis is one of the most segregated cities in America. There's a dividing line on Delmar Boulevard. North of the so-called Delmar Divide there is amazing community in the midst of dire economic poverty—and it's 95% black. To the south it's about 90% white. Downtown was a mix—gentrification next to homelessness. Attendance at the cathedral had been going down for a long time—people didn't want to come downtown. They thought they'd get shot, or accosted by people struggling with homelessness.

Then on Saturday August 9th 2014 a young man named Michael Brown was walking down the street in a part of St. Louis called Ferguson. A police officer named Darren Wilson pulled up next to him, wound down his window and told him to, "Get the fuck out of the street." That's the way the police talk to young black men and women, and gender non-conforming people in St. Louis. The only person alive today who knows exactly what went on that afternoon is Darren Wilson. But we do know that Mike Brown ended up dead and that his body lay in the street for four and a half hours.

What happened next was incredible. This community that had put up with police brutality and oppression over and over and over again, came out. They came out to mourn...and they came out for a candlelit vigil...and a peaceful march to the police department. The police responded with tear gas and dogs. And that's when this amazing group of young people found each other on the streets and on Twitter and they said, "No more—every time you kill one of us we step back but we're not standing down this time." It's the message of the activist Assata Shakur—*We have nothing to lose but our chains*.

Frankly, when I saw on Twitter that this person had been killed by the police I just thought, "Oh another one." But by Sunday a whole bunch of stuff had happened so I tore up the sermon I'd written and preached instead about Mike Brown and what was happening in our community. I was on a learning curve with all of this. My first response was typical of power, privilege and respectability—*We have to get these young people to calm down. We must talk reasonably about this.*

Then a few days later I was at a meeting with a group of clergy—because that week the clergy were having all these meetings—and we were sitting at a table in the sanctuary above the pews. We must have looked like a bunch of Pharisees. And a Pentecostal bishop named Derrick Robinson came in and said, "Don't tell the young people to get into your churches because they haven't been in them before, and they're not coming. You need to get out of here and onto the streets—listen to them and follow them. And don't wear your suits, wear your blue jeans." I remember this clearly as a watershed moment. My first thought was "Oh my God—he wants me to go out there. Does he get how *white* I am?" And my second thought was "Oh shit—he's right. I don't know how to do it or what I'm gonna do when I'm there but he's challenged me and that's exactly where I need to go." I've heard the cry of my people—this is Bartimaeus crying on the side of the road. I can't keep saying I believe these things if I don't go out there. And so that's when I started going out at night in Ferguson.

You must have been scared?

Oh hell—yeah. There were moments when shots were going off in various directions so I'd duck and run. But frankly I was mostly scared because I didn't know what my role was supposed to be and I didn't want to be stupid. And I'd spent five years at Christ Church Cathedral building relationships with people in power and authority like the police and I was scared of damaging those relationships and my respectability.

That first night out there I met Brittany Ferrell and Alexis Templeton—a woman and a non-binary person. They were standing arms linked with other people in front of the Ferguson Police Department and Brittany was screaming, "I am a person" at the police. I realised that my job in the community was to say, "What would you have us do for you?" like Jesus said to Bartimaeus. So whenever Brittany asked, "Do you have a space for us?" we'd open up the cathedral. On the first anniversary of Mike Brown's murder we held a huge non-violent resistance training.

I never met Mike Brown but he changed my life. Through his death I realised that I'd been living in a white world and that I was blinded to certain things because of my power and privilege. I'd been the white guy living in white St. Louis, with a couple of black friends and I'd thought of myself as a good white liberal. But I'd never before stepped outside that world so I'm eternally grateful that people like Brittany and Alexis let me stand with them.

I'm also grateful that I've been married to Robin for twenty-six years. She's a remarkable woman who knew how dangerous it was on the streets—and she totally understood why I had to go out there.

What did you learn about that world you stepped into?

I could go on and on about all the lessons of Ferguson and there is so much that my whole life I had just accepted. Like that you go one postcode across the Delmar Divide and you drop thirty years life expectancy. Our entire nation's economy was based on kidnapping black bodies from Africa, bringing them here and forcing labour out of them. That labour force gave us an amazing competitive advantage globally and we didn't want to give it up. So, as we've made some things illegal, we've just re-invented the slavery and oppression in new ways. When enslavement was eliminated in America, we did things like sharecropping and convict leasing, and now we have the school-to-prison pipeline and we shut people of colour out of the GI Bill and Social Security.

Then there's the redlining that limited black people buying houses in nice neighbourhoods. Those neighbourhoods are the ones where houses increase in value and that's the way most white Americans have built their wealth. It's still incredibly hard for people of colour to build wealth in America. The freedom that matters in this country is to be free to make as much money as you can. And that's what people in power in America care most about removing the chains from—that's what deregulation's all about. We still have an economy built on slavery and oppression. That's how capitalism works. And that's how we have Donald Trump as our president, right now. That's an affirmation that we're a conscienceless capitalist society.

I've heard a lot of people say that our policing system is broken. But it isn't broken. It's working just the way it was designed to. Policing in our country is about protecting white people and our property from black people and poor people and brown people. That's how it works. That's why one of the chants on the street was that the whole damn system is guilty as hell. But it doesn't have to be that way. It was no accident that the Magdalene St. Louis community for women was forming at the same time as all this happened. Because trauma-informed healing is the answer, and recognising that you need to focus on the voices that are crying out the most.

I was ashamed that these voices had been crying out for so long. And I'd heard some of them but felt I had more important things to do.

Did Ferguson change anything?

There was a moment in 2014 when the world was watching Ferguson, Missouri. That's amazing in itself. Think of a little nothing town where you live and then imagine it becoming a global household name. *Ferguson? Seriously?* What those young people did was to raise awareness of the reality of growing up black or brown in America today. Another thing is that not only were the leaders of that group young and black, they were also mostly lesbian, gay, bisexual, non-binary or transgender. They were on the outside in a number of ways and they inspired people in other parts of America...in Baltimore when Freddie Gray was murdered... and in Cleveland when Tamir Rice was murdered...and in Oakland and Los Angeles.

I remember when a cop in New York was charged with murdering Eric Garner—it was like *He murdered him. There's no doubt that he murdered him.* I sat at home watching CNN and saw these floods of people closing down the West Side Highway in New York, and it was surreal. I heard chants coming from my TV that had started in front of the Ferguson police department.

Frankly, I think a large factor in Trump's election was a backlash against what Ferguson ignited. Black people had the audacity to stand up and say, "I am a person" and white people said, "Huh. We're not gonna let you get away with that. We're gonna show you white supremacy. And we're gonna show it to you so you never stand up again. We're gonna *Make America Great Again.*"

On a personal level I've changed in a way that has made my life a lot harder and more complicated. Thank God. Because I can no longer buy into the capitalist, white supremacist narrative. I continue to live in it but I'm continually challenged to dismantle it and move beyond it.

As a priest I talk about the body of Christ a lot and the two places I've seen it in action are at Thistle Farms and Ferguson. Those amazing young people were not a faith-based movement at all but they were willing to lay down their lives for one another in the cause of love and justice. Black, brown, women, men, queer, non-binary—they stood together on the streets and that's what mattered. They said, "You can tell us to sit down but we're not sitting down ever again." Ferguson was this generation's Selma. I don't care how many people hate us now because I know that those young people are on the right side of history. And I hope that one day we're gonna be building statues of Brittany Ferrell and Alexis Templeton somewhere in St. Louis.

What do you hope to do now you are in Pasadena?

All Saints Church has this incredible history of being at the forefront of justice issues—of being bold and inclusive. That's one of the reasons I wanted to come here. But right now we're dealing with a lot of fear. We've a largely boomer congregation that's spent their entire lives being in control. Now as they move into retirement they see their power slipping away, and the millennials are the new generation. And here's this younger guy—I'm fifty and they think of me as young—coming in and centring all these other voices. I'd been told that one of the reasons the church wanted me was because of the experiences I'd had in St. Louis. As soon as I got here it was *Let's do this—let's bring these people in.* So I took them at their word and for six weeks we only had women of colour in the pulpit. And I've been trying to carve out the time to do more things with Black Lives Matter Pasadena, and with prisoners, and people who are struggling with homelessness. But we've had people in the congregation, particularly older white people, saying, "There's no place for *me* anymore."

I should have known better. I didn't realise the grief involved in transition. When you grow up in a non-privileged position you develop resilience to change. On the other hand when you grow up with power and wealth and privilege you have no resilience—you're not used to losing things. I've worked in communities in Ghana and Rwanda and South Sudan and what I've found is that the more people have, the less they think they have. It's counterintuitive. Wealth encourages us to look at everything in a zero-sum game kind of way—if the poor get more then there's less for me. But the thing is that love doesn't work that way. I can love you so much and it doesn't mean that I have to love anyone else any less. When you feel secure in a loving community then you don't have to worry about yourself. You know that everyone else is looking out for you and so you can fully centre on someone else.

I also forgot one of the core lessons of leadership which is that you've got to start by getting to know your community. You can lead people anywhere if you do it together. It's that old proverb—if you want to go fast go alone, if you want to go far go together. And we want to go far at All Saints.

So we've stepped back and we're talking about values and where we want to go, and most important of all is getting to know people in our big congregation, and building relationships. Churches tend to measure their success by the so-called ABC's of Empire—attendance, buildings and cash. But I want more for our church. What I want is for people to be able to say, "If my whole life fell apart I would go to All Saints—because I know that's the one community that would never reject me."

February 2019

Susan T

"Now I can look into the eyes of a mother whose child I'm burying and I can say, I understand—and they know that I do"

Mike copies me in on a warm email exchange in which he asks his friend Susan if she is interested in taking part. She agrees and I see from her response that she lives in St. Louis, Missouri and is a rabbi. In his handover, Mike tells me how much he admires Susan's justice work and says that "she is truly one of the most inspirational people in his life.'

We fix a time for a video call but Susan emails me the day before to say that there has been a death in her congregation and she needs to be with the family. We rearrange for a few days later.

When we do get to talk there is no shortage of topics to cover. Susan is a feminist and activist. She tells me about the public challenges she has faced and what it was like to be in the early wave of American female rabbis. We also talk about the hardest challenge of all. It's so huge that it's there right from the beginning. We've just started the call when Susan looks beyond me and focuses on the wall of my study. It's a deep red. "My daughter's wall was painted that colour," she says. "It was her favourite."

What are the main things that are going on for you right now, Susan?

Well I guess the first thing I need to mention is that my youngest daughter died about sixteen months ago. I've seen grief in other people and thought I could feel their pain but really I had no idea what it's like. It takes up a lot of space. My daily work right now is figuring out a way to live without my daughter and with my grief. And somehow to find a balance and expand into something more.

Adina loved New York. It's where she lived and worked. She was a prize-winning writer and the managing editor of *One Story Magazine*. She wrote about bias and difference, and she touched many lives—there is already a fellowship for new writers established in her name. Things are coming out of this tragedy, for sure but none of it really helps. She was just thirty-one when she died.

I'm doing a lot of the same things that I did before Adina died but I do them in a different way. Now I can look into the eyes of a mother whose child I'm burying and I can say, "I understand." And they know that I do.

How do you know Mike?

It was through both being involved in the Ferguson Uprising—the movement for black lives here in St. Louis. We were together on the streets and we saw these young people emerge as leaders, especially these beautiful, young, queer people. They would look into the police officers' eyes and say, "Look at me. Look at me—I'm a human being, I'm a mother, I'm a student..." They were coming from the margins and claiming their space in the world. That's the kind of thing my daughter wrote about. Mike and I fell in love with these young people and so we kept going out night after night onto the streets. We ended up doing a lot of mothering. And he mothered as much as anybody! I learned so many things from that time.

Can you tell me about them...

Well, one came out of the fact that the young Ferguson protesters identified with kids in Gaza. There was tear gas here and rubber bullets, and the Gaza kids were texting with advice about how to deal with them and how to deal with militarised police. I felt I was there to stand in solidarity with these young people and to protect them. But I was also asked, "What side are you going to stand on Rabbi? We know you care about black lives. Do you care about Palestinian lives?" I'm a Progressive Zionist rabbi. That means that I believe with all my heart that Israel has the right to exist but I also care deeply about justice for the Palestinians and I'm still hoping that we haven't gone too far for a two-state solution. Things became very messy. But I've been showing up for racial justice in this city for over thirty years so I was not new to this fight and I had real friends on the street. I was included in everything by the black community because *Of course Susan has to be here. She's family*. I heard that again and again and yet there was still this tension.

It's been a long, complicated story but in short, I'm leaving for Israel and Palestine this coming Monday. We're a group of women—three rabbis and three Christian clergy that were involved in Ferguson and we're going so we can experience what's happening there. We've been talking about it for a while. We were supposed to go two years ago but Adina was very sick with lymphoma then, so we couldn't.

There was another important thing that happened. It was July when she got ill, and in September we had a second uprising in St. Louis following the killing of another young, black man. He probably needed a warrant or a slap on the wrist—not to be shot by a police officer. But that's what happened and Stockley the police officer was not indicted for his killing. That caused a huge night of protest in St. Louis and because we'd already had Ferguson a few years before, it wasn't just people of color who were protesting. Many white people had done *Witnessing Whiteness* classes and were engaged in racial justice work. There were thousands of people in the crowd and it was really diverse. The first night of the protest was a Friday night and as I was finishing services in our synagogue we looked out of the big windows and saw the protesters coming down the street. They were our friends. So we were all waving to each other in support. And then all of a sudden the police blocked the street and came at the protestors from both sides with tear gas and rubber bullets. The protesters had nowhere to go so we threw open the doors of the synagogue and said, "Come in. Come in. You'll be safe here—you're our guests." We were ready for this because in the Ferguson Uprising we always said that we'd stay open through the night to be a sanctuary and provide things like triage, water and bathrooms. Many of the people had never been inside a synagogue before but we got them in and then I went out with my co-rabbi and we said to the police, "Look, they're our guests—we're going to keep them safe." And they said, "You keep them in there and we'll leave them alone. But if they come out we'll arrest them." So we stayed till about two in the morning and it was an important night.

My daughter died in January a few months later, on the Friday before the Martin Luther King birthday weekend. That weekend is always a big deal in America. It's a public holiday on the Monday and there are lots of marches and other events. Unfortunately, the way it turned out, that Monday was the only time we could have her funeral and I just had to think, "OK, it's just what it is."

One of my closest friends is the Reverend Traci Blackmon of the United Church of Christ. She's a very dear woman and has become a national figure and leader for racial justice. I didn't even know at the time but that Monday she was supposed to be preaching in California with Harry Belafonte at some huge Dr. King thing. But she knew I needed her at the funeral so she came and sang *Amazing Grace*. When she sang it was like the heavens opened. There were over a thousand people in the synagogue so it was hard to see much but I looked up and outside those windows, I saw my protester family. They'd left all their Dr. King stuff and they were standing there. They came to my daughter's funeral and they came to the shiva. They baked and they were so loving and so tender.

Adina died a terribly violent death to chemotherapies that are very primitive and on their way out. She only just missed out on the new immunotherapies. But we had a lot of privilege in our lives, and this group of people who live on the edge every day, showed up for me in a way I will never forget. They know what it is to lose their children to gun violence. When their black sons leave the house they don't know if they are ever going to come home again. And some days when I think I don't want to live because I miss Adina so much, I think about what other people are living with. These parents that have lost children from violence—they are kids that didn't need to die. The word that keeps coming to me on this journey is *humility*. How dare I think that I have a right to give up. My daughter never gave up. It takes time but I'm slowly coming back to my life and doing things like teaching and visiting people in the hospital—in cancer wards, too, though this is still very hard. And I'm doing a lot of weddings. Some are for my daughter's friends. I can't say no—I did their baby namings when they were babies. They're important as well, because you know in our tradition if a wedding party and a funeral meet in the street, the funeral procession stops and the wedding goes ahead.

What led to you becoming a rabbi?

When I was growing up in the 50s and 60s there were no women rabbis. There had been a woman called Regina Jonas who was ordained in Germany in 1935 but she died in Auschwitz and it wasn't until 1972 that the first woman rabbi, Sally Priesand, was ordained in America. In some ways this was nothing new as throughout history there have been women who've served and done this work. But they weren't called rabbis and their voices were very quiet.

I was at college in 1972 and head of a feminist group there. I'd invite various women to come and speak to us and one of them was Betty Friedan who wrote *The Feminine Mystique*. She was one of my heroes. After her wonderful talk we were having coffee with her and she asked us what we wanted to be. She saw my Jewish star and said, "What are you going to do—be a rabbi?" And I said, "No. The last thing I want to be is a token in a patriarchal tradition. Never!"

Anyway, I graduated from college in 1974 and went to work on an archaeological dig in Carthage, Tunisia. I was planning to do some kind of graduate program in Near Eastern Studies or Greek and Roman Studies so that I could teach and do archaeology. Then while I was back home doing some applications, I bumped into a rabbi that I'd grown up with. He was with his wife and they both said to me, "You should apply to rabbinical school, you know. We're looking for women." I said, "*Rabbinical* school? Come *on*!" But when I looked into it, I started to think, "OK, it's five years but it's a great education, and I'm already on a spiritual journey." So I applied.

I forgot about it and then I got called for an interview. It didn't go very well. They asked me some sexist questions like "What happens if a male congregant makes a pass at you?" And I said, "Do you ask the men that question?" When I was just about to leave, one of the older rabbis looked at me and said, "What is your favourite book in English literature?" He was from Europe and talked very, very slowly. I'd just finished reading *Ivanhoe* and I loved it—I think I read it five times. So we got into this amazing conversation about *Ivanhoe* and it must have made an impression because they accepted me.

I was back in Carthage when I heard and I had to get to Tel Aviv to start right away. Because it was on my passport that I'd been in Tunisia and a number of other Arab countries I had to jump through all sorts of hoops. At Rome Airport, I was asked, "Why are you going to Israel?" and when I said, "I'm going to be a rabbi," they said, "*What*? There's no such thing as a woman rabbi." Anyway, I finally made it to Israel and on the first day I met a fellow student who would later become my husband.

Every day I thank God for that chance moment that led to me becoming a rabbi. Because together with my husband and children, this work is the love of my life. People let you into their lives at the most tender times and you get to have real relationships with them.

What happened after you finished rabbinical school?

My husband and I were together in Cincinnati and when we were about to be ordained I said, "Let's do something that nobody's done before. Let's share a rabbi job. We'll share work, childcare, housework—everything." A lot of people offered us a job but it was for either him or me. Then a rabbi in St. Louis offered us what we wanted. One salary for the two of us to share. We thought that was so revolutionary but it ended up that the synagogue was getting two for one. There wasn't a model for it, and I didn't have maternity leave because they'd never had to think about that before. And then I found that once you start nursing a baby, you're not sharing anymore. So we learned that we had different skills and although we loved the people there, it was a suburban congregation which wasn't what I wanted. So we both left.

What are the guiding principles of your work?

Thirty-five years ago when other Jewish congregations were moving to the suburbs I got together with a group of people to found a congregation that was committed to staying in the city. That's where the racial justice issues are, and we wanted to be part of the solution not part of white flight. We rented a church for sixteen years, and then we were able to build our own synagogue. It's in a very prominent place and people tell us we're the most vulnerable space in the city. But I was with a police officer the other day who said, "Susan, you're in the 'hood. We're gonna make sure nothing bad happens to you." That was really sweet—a black police officer saying that.

For me, life is about relieving suffering, and serving. Every day I get to do that, and it's not just with Jews. We've worked hard to become an inclusive and integrated community—to open our congregation to the LGBTQ community and to Jews of color who really had no place to go, and to make sure that Jews in interfaith families and converts to Judaism don't find themselves on the outside.

When Adina died I had to say where people could donate. Of course I thought of the hospitals that had cared for her, and of *One Story* where she worked and cared so much about literature, writing, creativity, feminism and difference. But I also said, "Maybe we should create an Adina Fund for Early Childhood Education." Every study says that if you want to change culture, do it through early childhood education. And so now we have a daycare centre at the synagogue—we call it The Nest. We want to create an egalitarian, feminist, democratic, educational experience for babies and preschool children.

What was it like, being one of the first women rabbis?

When I first came to St. Louis there was another woman rabbi here but she was at the university. She was a very traditional woman with a good background in Jewish thought and Jewish texts. And that was probably a good thing because she broke down some stereotypes before I came. But I was the first congregational rabbi and that was a challenge. There were people who didn't want me to do their life cycle events because that wouldn't be *real*. And we're all talking about *me too* now. I had lots of *me too moment*s but I didn't know how to name them in those days. I knew that people were using my gender against me and that it was largely about power, and about people feeling threatened because maybe if I was important in their lives it would change the balance of power in their homes and workplaces. That was when it began to really matter to me to change the culture in the workplace so that women could be seen for their whole selves and not have their gender used as a weapon against them. I didn't have any role models in the synagogue but I did seek out Christian women clergy because they'd already been through this. Some of those women are still my closest friends.

One of the biggest surprises for me was that my first battles were with women. With the men, there was a lot of baloney. But with the women, there was stupid stuff like feeling I was a threat to them because of how I looked, or the length of my skirt, or whether I wore hose or not. I soon began to realise that I needed to gain the trust of the other women and to let them know that this was not an ego thing for me. I wasn't looking for attention. I was looking for real relationships. And I worked hard at using my power to make space for women's voices—to not let men overpower meetings, for example.

That prepared me for Ferguson, too. Many of the churches where I was asked to speak, don't have women clergy. Mike won't speak in places where they don't make space for women and I had to do the same thing for women of colour. A lot of my work was learning what it really means to be an ally to women—how to keep my mouth shut and how not to take up too much space with my privilege but to demand and hold that space for women of colour, especially for my clergy sisters.

What shaped you?

The first things I think of are my mother and the love I got from both of my parents. When you're loved that much you feel like you can do anything. You want to give it back and to pay it forward. That's the kind of mother I wanted to be. But I was also doing this big job, so I hope my kids would say that I was. Adina had a heart transplant when she was nineteen and nothing was more important than making sure that she got well. The cancer was different. It was so much harder and I don't know if we made the right decisions. I hope she knew that I would have done anything for her.

So I guess the thing that has shaped me the most is loving my kids and being a mother to them. That's one of the hard things now. In the past I would spill myself out all day because I had to, and the thought of getting home to my husband and three kids would keep me going. Since losing Adina I keep trying to remember that feeling. I'm lucky to still have my husband and two children and I also have a three-year old grandson who is such a joy. You love your kids but this is a different kind of love. It opens your heart. But I lost Adina just as I got him so I guess I'm shaped by both love and loss.

What does it mean to you to be a Jewish woman?

A lot of religious traditions are about being *either, or*. And I understand that proselytising and evangelism—if you have something that you love so much then you want to give it to other people. But for me, being a Jewish woman is about holding space for the most vulnerable. For those who walk a different walk or have a different song in their head, or are good in their own way. We all have different garments but beneath those garments is the soul and that's the same for all of us. I want to live in a world where we can trust each other and not have to be the same. To me that's the essence of Judaism.

And what do you want to do next?

Well, I'm sixty-six years old and I have to choose to live every day now without my daughter. And I'm also feeling very acutely that I have to figure out what's next. One of the names for God is *HaMakom* which means *a place*—I have to work out what my place is. How do I take what I've learned and make space for the next generation, and find ways to support them as we continue to fight injustice. In America I don't know how we sleep at night. We're keeping children in detention camps at our border. It's a terrible thing because they're brown—so it's racist. We'll be paying for that in generations to come. A few months ago, on the one-year anniversary of Adina's death, I went to Guatemala with the American Jewish World Service. A couple of children had died on the border, and I wanted to see what life was like in Guatemala and what made people risk everything to come here. It feels like that's another thing in my life that I need to pay attention to, because now I know. And once you know, you have to do something. You have to act.

So there's all of that. Or is my place to help my children with their children and be a full-time grandma? It might be. I could balance that with teaching them that their grandmother is an activist and a feminist. I want to respond to what's in front of me but I also want to honour those who will come after me, and those who've gone before me—my mother and those other Jewish women whose shoulders I stand on. I'm still trying to figure it all out.

May 2019

Ruth

"I decided to run for political office—I wanted to understand who was making these decisions and see if I could do it better"

Once again I find myself being copied in on a warm email exchange and am delighted when Ruth agrees to take part and tells Susan that "This is the most lovely approach to tell social change stories that I have read about, ever." Later when I email her direct she replies positively saying that "the project sounds totally fascinating."

Ruth lives in New York and Susan says she is one of her heroes—"and a force of nature!" That sounds a bit daunting and during several email exchanges to arrange our video call I discover that she doesn't waste time on unnecessary words. "Would 8am your time be OK?" I ask. Back comes the succinct answer 'perfect.'

This time I do a bit of reading beforehand and discover that in 1997 Ruth was the first woman to receive the Democratic nomination for New York City mayor and ran against Rudy Giuliani. She has received numerous accolades for her work, was featured in the Jerusalem Post's list of the 'World's Most Influential Jews' and has made repeated appearances in The Forward's list of '50 Most Influential Jews of the Year.' At the age of 78, she continues to be a tireless activist and advocate for social justice.

When we talk, she couldn't be more helpful. And she says something that gives me particular pause for thought—"I've increasingly come to appreciate that the hardest thing is to **really** *listen to people." That's something I'm discovering, too and it has been a surprise. I'd thought that I've listened attentively in each interview but time and time again as I've transcribed the interviews, I've found that I missed important nuances. By listening to the conversations again, I've gained a much better understanding of what the interviewees were* **really** *saying. It's been a privilege not available during normal conversation and it has made me wonder how much I miss in* *my everyday interactions—how much we all miss.*

It's the start of the day for Ruth when we chat, and she gives a masterclass in multi-tasking—she eats her breakfast, shuffles some papers, gives sartorial advice to her granddaughter, and all the while I never once doubt that I have her attention.

How did you get into public life, Ruth?

The overriding theme for me has always been the pursuit of social justice. That's a basic Jewish teaching and it's followed me throughout my life. As a teenager I got involved with the settlement house movement and I think it was through seeing poor children that I was inspired to pursue a degree in social work.

Initially I thought I'd do individual case work but then I became much more interested in influencing social change through community projects. One was working with and for, a group of parents who were starting a small alternative school on the West Side. That was in 1968 and at that time the local schools were significantly segregated by race and class, even though the school hierarchy denied that. We set our school up to be different. It was run by parents for children in the neighborhood—one-third black, one-third white, and one-third Hispanic. I think that the children benefited tremendously from the time they spent there—the poorer children, those of colour and the ones with significant learning challenges on the one hand and those who were for the first time encountering the diversity of their own neighborhood, on the other hand.

Around the same time there were lots of housing battles going on in my neighborhood on Manhattan's West Side. It's about four blocks by fifty blocks and compared to many cities, it had a mixed population. Some avenues had fancy apartment buildings but there were also side streets with small town houses that had originally been for a single family and had been carved up over the years into much smaller apartments. These were home to lots and lots of people from a range of ethnic and racial backgrounds.

Then the City of New York came up with an urban renewal plan for a twenty square block in the area. That sounds like a really good thing but in this case, as too often, urban renewal meant urban removal. So they'd say, "We're gonna fix up this neighborhood and there'll be housing for everybody. We're sorry that we'll have to knock down the houses in which *you people* live but when we build new buildings you'll be able to come back." And that just wasn't true because the City was making no real provisions for that to happen.

I knew many of those families whose housing was being torn down, and there were plenty of real estate people ready to build smart new apartment blocks in their place. A local priest led the battle to protect housing for those who had been the original tenants, and for a number of years we fought the City at every level to ensure that 20-30% of the new apartments were set aside for that group of our neighbors. The outcome is that whilst this neighborhood certainly still has its fancier streets, and I'm not denying that I live on one of them, as a *whole* it's more integrated by race and class than most other gentrifying neighborhoods.

So those were two projects that I was proud to work on, and there were plenty of others—race, racism, voting rights and immigration have always been big issues. Over and over again I saw Government leaders and bureaucrats denying justice to those in the greatest need of good homes and decent schools. They openly discriminated on the basis of race and class, and all of that inspired me to do something that I'd never imagined. I decided to run for political office because I wanted to understand who was making these decisions and see if I could do it better. The upshot was that I ended up being in New York City Government for twenty years.

What did you work on in Government?

I worked on some of those same issues of race, poverty, homelessness, public education and public higher education. But you have to be able to tell people how the government can pay for these things, so I also became something of an expert on tax programmes in the City.

There's no escaping that the economy in New York City is based on its real estate. And over the years, the real estate industry had been able to negotiate many tax breaks for itself and hang on to them all. So, for example, they'd tell the Government that they wanted to build a fifty-storey office block or renovate run down buildings into new and improved housing, and whatever it was, they'd argue that they couldn't do it unless they had some tax forgiveness. For many years I exposed those programs and challenged the Government—"Why on earth are you giving someone a tax break to build in the middle of Manhattan?" Recently, Channel 4 made a series about Donald Trump and you can see an old clip on that where I'm arguing with him about tax breaks being a gift to developers and depriving the City of needed revenue.

That was one area of work. Another was electoral reform and as a result of that New York City now has the best city campaign finance laws in the country. We have limits on how many terms people can serve in office, but more importantly we have a system in which small donor gifts are matched heavily by the City of New York. So in effect, taxpayers help to fund campaigns, and that allows less well-off people to run and helps to level the playing field between and among candidates. I'm proud of my role in this as it's an increasingly big issue in America. Another thing I helped to introduce was protected roadways so that it's now possible to roller skate, bike or walk almost perfectly around the island of Manhattan.

Then in 1997 things changed—I ran in an unlikely-to-be-successful race for mayor, campaigning mostly to improve public education, and I lost. After that it took a little bit of time to figure out what to do next.

And what *did* you do?

Some unbelievable happenstance led me to the American Jewish World Service (AJWS), an organisation that supports efforts to end poverty and expand human rights in the non-Jewish developing world—all done according to Jewish values. It was very small when I joined as CEO but it grew tremendously during the time I ran it, and it's become very successful. I learned a lot from the people who worked with me, about how to do that kind of development work. One of the important things is that we pay full attention to the dignity of the people with whom we work, respecting their visions of justice and funding them to do the work that they want to do.

Just over two years ago I stepped down from running AJWS and the person who had come on board nine years before as the executive vice president took over. That was great for me because he kept me on in a part-time role to continue to work on global social justice issues. I push all kinds of people in the Jewish community to be interested in global work—rabbis, rabbinical students and general audiences—and I represent AJWS in interfaith efforts as well. It's important to do this because otherwise people push global issues out of their consciousness. We have a cohort of rabbis of all different backgrounds whom we pick to work with us every year and they take our message back to their communities.

And I might add that because I now work only part-time for AJWS, I work in other more local endeavors as well and address other pressing issues of our time like race, racism, immigration and voting rights.

How does the American Jewish World Service work?

When I was in City Government I used an inclusive approach. So instead of saying, "We'll sit in City Hall and decide what the Lower East Side needs," I'd say, "Why don't we go out to the people on the Lower East Side and ask *them* what they need." And when I went to AJWS the philosophy there was entirely in parallel with that.

We work in many different situations around the world where an indigenous leader has stepped forward and said they want to fight on behalf of a marginalised population. So it could be land or water rights, for example, or keeping girls in school, or reproductive and sexual rights. And when we talk about marginalised populations, that's a huge number of people. Women are marginalised in many countries and LGBT people are too. Right now we work in nineteen countries and fund about five hundred grass roots organisations and social movements.

During my time with AJWS we've probably funded about two thousand projects and we've worked very closely with many of the leaders of these organisations. Probably the most famous is Leymah Gbowee who led *Women of Liberia Mass Action for Peace*. Across religious and ethnic lines, she organised Christian and Muslim women to oppose the highly corrupt government and its engagement in a meaningless but destructive civil war. Under Leymah's leadership the women staged a sex strike, and they surrounded the building in

Ghana where the parties were supposedly negotiating. Basically, they demanded an end to the war—and they won. Leymah was awarded the Nobel Peace Prize for her efforts, together with Ellen Johnson Sirleaf the President of Liberia. That's one dramatic example of leaders that we've supported.

Another is Eliana Elías in Peru. She came from a nice, upstanding family and went to a nice Catholic school but thirty years ago she decided to spend her life with indigenous people in the Amazon, the most remote region of her country. She founded an organisation that has had spectacular success, particularly in helping women learn about their own bodies and reproductive health and in empowering those women to take control of their lives—fighting domestic violence, investing in the future of their children and starting small businesses. I continue to work with her as a consultant and friend.

Then there's a woman in Guatemala who grew up poor but went to law school and now advises smallholder indigenous farmers on their land rights and how to hold onto their farms. I see her every year and in 2018 we took a group of rabbis to Guatemala to see the range of local organisations fighting for their own human rights. These rabbis were a cohort of our Global Justice Fellowship, a six-month programme designed to inspire and train American rabbis so that they can lead their communities in advocating for human rights around the world. Rabbi Susan Talve was part of that cohort. I'd heard about her work in Ferguson and knew that she was the kind of rabbi who was always willing to stick her neck out for justice. So I persuaded her to join the programme. That was the year after her daughter died—it was tough for her, but she's an amazing person and we became close.

What has been hardest in your working life?

There's been a lot that's exciting and challenging but I've increasingly come to appreciate that the hardest thing is to really listen to people. It's easy to go and do things for people that they haven't asked for. You can feel good about yourself until you realise that it hasn't been useful. It's also a little too easy to say, "We'd like to help you. Write us a proposal." And then to not lend them the right kind of critical ears and eyes that makes the proposal better without substituting our judgement for their judgement—to work with humility and with full respect for the other person. If the solution to the problems in the Global South could come from Washington, London, Geneva or New York, we'd be over these problems already. But the solutions are being invented and practised at the grass roots level and that's where we need to support people. At AJWS we use the phrase, *Nothing about us without us*.

Then another hard thing is when you run into people who don't see things as you do, and can't see any reason to change. The ongoing challenge is to listen to people but also to figure out what you can do to convince them to think differently. I feel very strongly about the issue of immigration and am astounded when Jewish individuals or organisations don't agree. When I speak with them I say, "Look at the Jewish community. Immigration has been the story of our lives as a people for six thousand years. We should be able to engage more people with more energy and leadership on this issue."

Right now there are seventy million immigrants and refugees in the world, and every country is handling them relatively badly, often motivated by fear of the unknown and by a lack of appreciation for the situations that have made those people flee their own countries in the first place. Over the past decade it's been Germany that's handled them best but now Angela Merkel is in real trouble precisely for trying to provide refuge to people in need. Parts of the Jewish community in America want refugee families to take care of but I want them to be fighting to change immigration *policy*. Shifting people from service and caring to policy advocacy is a big challenge. It's the same with environmental issues. We can talk about what to compost and which bin to put things in at the synagogue, but more importantly we need to change our national dependence on fossil fuels and we need to rejoin with other countries as part of the Paris Agreement to slow down the rate of climate change.

Have you ever felt scared or threatened by any of the positions you've had to take?

Oh yeah. I've certainly been in some weird places where I was afraid. I've never been threatened but there were times when it was a little dangerous and it wasn't quite clear how an American woman would be treated. But I want to put that in perspective. During my time at American Jewish World Service we had several grass roots environmental leaders and LGBT campaigners who were murdered because of their work. Berta Caceres was one of our activists in Honduras and was shot at her door by thugs. They'd been hired by a hydroelectric dam construction company.

I've never been scared or threatened in that way but part of what I try to teach is how to get people to develop their leadership skills and to have moral courage and be willing to take risks on behalf of what they believe. I think that's relevant to your question. Yesterday when I was talking to young social activists I was on a panel with two quite distinguished people and I was struck how both of them kept modifying their sentences—*You might want to...* and *We could think about...* and *Some of you will...* In contrast I thought, "I don't have time for this. If you're here it's because you want to make change and if you want to make change there are going to be lots of times where you'll have to speak truth to power." So I spoke more in that vein, urging them to take a stand and to speak truth to power.

I saw an example of that recently with a rabbi at an event where the keynote speaker, a Government official, was saying that the problems at our US borders are being exaggerated. The speaker was still on the stage when the rabbi said a prayer before dinner. She spoke truth to power when she said that each of us with our different faiths knows that it's wrong to put children in cages. It's so easy to give a perfectly good speech but not to challenge the people you're talking to—she was willing to take the bigger risk.

How do your upbringing and your Jewish faith influence your work?

Significantly, in a couple of different ways. One important thing is that my mother worked full-time unlike most of the other mothers my sister and I knew. So we had a very different role model for taking up our places in the world. Also, she was a public relations director for a rabbinic seminary and was an incredible pioneer. She helped to get the message out about Conservative Judaism and how it spoke to issues of ethics and justice, gender equity, and the environment. One of the things she did was to co-produce NBC's *The Eternal Light* on radio and then television. From 1944 for over four decades it used Jewish themes, Jewish history and Jewish values to broadcast programmes that were sometimes just informational but sometimes contained powerful messages of moral and spiritual courage. That's some of what we breathed at home.

I also think it was significant that there was just my sister and me. It was a time when everybody was happy to have a girl—so long as they also had a boy. My father probably invested more energy in his daughters because he did not have a son and because he had respect for my mother as a professional. My sister and I grew up assuming that we could work full-time, raise a family, and take care of everything. It's not like our parents shared household responsibilities. My sister became a paediatrician, and she and I agreed a few years ago that we could never remember our father having washed a dish. But the implication was that it's OK—women can do it all.

With regard to my Jewish faith, I need to go back a bit further to answer that. My paternal grandfather was an immigrant who set up a successful silver and china retail business. My father knew about Jewish rituals and celebrations but I don't think he grew up with a clear religious framework—it seemed to me that his family was more focused on issues of class than issues of faith. My mother was raised by a committed Jewish father but a mother who felt strongly about assimilation—*Judaism was for the old country, now we can be Americans as opposed to Jews.*

When my mother got to college she decided that she wanted to understand Judaism better and she set about doing that. Then she needed a job in order to support my father through graduate school because, although he was the eldest son, he had turned down the family business and was training to be a certified public accountant. She ended up working for the Jewish Theological Seminary of America, and she learned Judaism on the job. She and my father set up a home that was probably more Jewish than the ones that either of them had grown up in. We weren't Orthodox and we didn't keep kosher, and people rarely talked about their beliefs but we did celebrate Jewish holidays and my parents' values centered around social justice and philanthropy. That didn't so much mean giving money—they didn't have a lot of disposable cash. What they did was to give huge amounts of time to lay service in Jewish organisations. All that was passed on to me and my sister.

I like to think I carried that into my adult professional life and passed it on to my own family. But I don't think it was obvious in my political life. I didn't do much talking in the Jewish community and to be quite blunt, at that time I'd say that the established Jewish community in New York was not doing nearly enough to think about its role in the city. It wasn't asking, "What's our role in a divided city? What's our role with regard to black people? What are additional ways we can put our faith into action?" So I did work on these issues during my time in government but only occasionally did I talk about it coming from my faith. I was much more likely to speak about Judaism if I was invited to speak at the funeral of a non-Jewish community activist. Then I'd talk about the importance in my tradition of the values you leave behind and the people you've influenced.

When I got the job at American Jewish World Service it opened up all kinds of horizons for me. It took me into new settings that were very exciting and introduced me to some wonderful people who were making social change, many of them women. I was doing it for a Jewish organisation and that made perfect sense to me because I see it as quintessentially Jewish to care about child brides in India even though they aren't Jewish, and quintessentially Jewish to let farmers in El Salvador tell us how we can help *them* instead of us telling them what they need to do. These are Jewish concepts and as I built AJWS, I hired rabbis and Jewish educators who helped shape my understanding of how to make these connections and speak about them publicly.

Can you tell me about your mayoral campaign?

Yes, sure. I was up against Rudy Giuliani who was running for a second term, and I had a wonderful group of people who worked with me on the campaign, as well as a vast army of volunteers. But there were disappointments along the way and I learned that the people you think are your friends are not always there for you. Some people hedged their bets and wanted to back the winner. Giuliani had done some good things in his first term as Mayor but he had also neglected many of the important issues in the life of the city, particularly when it came to poor people.

It was reasonable to challenge him but as much as ten months before the election it was clear that he probably couldn't be beaten, and it was certainly clear that *I* couldn't beat him. That led some people who I just assumed would be there every minute fighting the good fight with me, to say things like, "Maybe you should drop out...I really can't afford to do this...my union has to be on the winning side...I can give you 2,000 dollars but I'm giving the mayor 20,000 dollars..." But what upset and surprised me most of all, was getting that from the New York press. All too often their attitude was, "Why should we cover what he says and you say on an equal basis when we know he's gonna win?" And I'd say, "Excuse me, I can't reach nine million people in New York. It's your job in a democratic election to tell them that I believe differently from him." That was my argument, but it did not carry the day.

What do you think are the biggest issues facing the US right now?

One is related to what I've just been talking about. Donald Trump has dramatically contributed to people having no idea where the truth comes from. His steady attacks on the press and his disregard for the truth influence too much of the general public who then don't know who or what to believe.

Jeff Bezos owns the *Washington Pos*t and when Trump got elected he changed the masthead to say *Democracy Dies in Darkness*. A bold move. But even though it's a powerful voice, he's just one voice and one newspaper. I was at a conference with a progressive rabbi recently and when I said some things about the rest of the world, he asked where he could get good information. You'll be happy to know that I said, "Read *The Guardian*. And watch BBC Television. At least they actually know there are 160 countries in the world and they tell you what's happening."

That reminds me of when my daughter was volunteering in Peru, thirty years ago. There was guerrilla warfare going on there and so I had every reason to worry about her. When I asked someone what I should do, they said, "Buy *The Wall Street Journal* every day because if there's a problem in Peru, investors will want to know." And it was true. *The New York Times* didn't cover Peru, but every so often *The Wall Street Journal* would mention some piece of information and warn investors, and I could use that to determine if my daughter was in new danger.

Another issue is that the US has built a country by killing Native Americans, and stealing land from them without acknowledging the depths of its racism. Many of the countries I've come across in my international work have had horrendous splits, civil wars and genocides, but many have done a better job of facing up to their history than the US has. Our track record on these fronts is quite poor. That said, I note with surprise that in our current crazy presidential race candidates are being asked what they think about the issue of reparations. That doesn't mean that we're going to provide them but it's not inconceivable to me that in the next twelve years we could elect an American president who will apologise for the deep racist roots in this country.

Then there are the issues that connect so many of us in America, the UK, on the Continent and some places in the Global South—the important but occasionally shaky value of patriotism is being replaced by out and out nationalism and nativism. That's terrifying. I don't pretend to know where it comes from, and I certainly don't know what to do about it. But I have a couple of bon mots that I find useful. One is *Despair is not a strategy*. The other is *We can't retreat to the convenience or the luxury of being overwhelmed*.

I'm not saying that people can't be overwhelmed—I feel overwhelmed myself several times a day. I just have to read the headlines. What I mean is that lots of us have significant privilege. And with that privilege comes responsibility. Many of the leaders I've worked with through AJWS, step out every morning with their vision of justice and almost no resources. There's no certainty that they're going to succeed and they're often in dangerous situations. When you work with those kind of people then it makes you think, “If that's what they're doing every day, then is there something more that I should be doing?”

What are you proudest of?

That one's easy—my children. All three are serious about their professions and their Judaism and they're all significantly engaged in social justice work. That's quite satisfying. But I guess I'm also proud that I've been able to keep a consistent focus on the kind of change I want to make in the world. Even when it's not immediately successful and it takes a long time and is full of frustrations.

July 2019

John

"Ending genocide is a life calling for me—it goes back to when I was thirteen years old"

My next interviewee lives in Houston. Ruth says that she is delighted to e-introduce me to John. She calls him an amazing Renaissance man with a deep passion for justice, as well as being a very unusual and successful business leader. She adds that he is more conscious of his actions then anyone else she knows.

John replies to my email promptly and asks his executive assistant Laura to arrange the video call. We have a couple of friendly exchanges and agree a date. In the meantime I discover that John started his business Bridgeway Capital Management twenty-six years ago, and that the firm's mission statement includes the phrase—a commitment to ending genocide. As John says himself, this is a bit unusual for a financial services firm and when we get to talk, it quickly becomes clear that this is no ordinary business.

How did you become committed to ending genocide?

I promise you that most normal people if they're not Jewish with a history of the Holocaust or not Rwandan, they don't wake up in the morning thinking about ending genocide. And it's not a very happy or pretty cause. But it's a life calling for me and goes back to when I was thirteen years old. I was studying World War II in a history class and we came across a description of the Holocaust. Now, I grew up in a happy home and the parenting style of that generation was to give your kids a joyful childhood and keep the hard stuff from them. So I'd never heard anything about the Holocaust before and nor had most of my friends. I read it and I thought, "This must be wrong. I can't believe that people would let this happen." It didn't resonate with how I was raised. But I reflected on it quite a while and thought, "Well it happened once, and it's history, and at least now that we know, we'll never let it happen again." I bought hook, line and sinker into that saying *Never again.*

Then when I was nineteen years old, the Cambodian genocide happened. And that was such a shock. I remember thinking, "What happened to never again? I thought this wasn't ever gonna happen again. And what are people doing about it?" The Holocaust had seemed like ancient history to a thirteen year-old boy but the Cambodian genocide was happening in my lifetime, on my watch, and I felt helpless. And I couldn't think what a nineteen year-old could actually do about it.

By the time the Rwandan genocide happened in 1994 I was more spiritually mature. The whole thing kicked off when a plane was shot out of the sky with the presidents of Rwanda and Burundi on board. I knew that Rwanda was in Africa but that was about all I could have told you and I couldn't even have pointed it out on a map. But then I found myself reading the *Wall Street Journal* and a five sentence report about the plane crash. I kept staring at it and had no idea why. It was sad, a plane went down, two people died, they were world leaders... That's all that was there in those sentences but for some reason I felt a strong connection. And then over the next few days everything broke loose in Rwanda and there were four months of conflagration. By this time I had a very different view of the world and knew that it was possible to do something. We have pictures looking down on the earth from outer space and there are no national borders. There just aren't any. They're all man-made—there's a commonness of humanity and the whole earth is our backyard.

That year 1994, was when I started *Bridgeway Capital Management*. My wife and I both grew up in very comfortable homes but we didn't aspire to a lot of wealth. I'd seen some of the dangers of being sucked into money, power and possessions and by this time we'd achieved the level of material wealth that we wanted. We didn't want to just consume more and we thought that giving some of our money away would help address that problem. So one of our founding principles was to give back half of our net profits to charitable and non-profit organisations through the *Bridgeway Foundation* which is the philanthropic arm of our business. These include projects to end genocide and war atrocities throughout the world. But ten years after founding *Bridgeway* I realised that our goal was naive. We've been able to attract extraordinary people who want to stay long-term because of what we do and how we do it. And that has made a very successful business. But it hasn't really solved our problem—the half that's left over is bigger than what we would have had if we'd not done it this way!

Can you tell me about your efforts to end genocide and war atrocities...

It takes a long time to establish relationships in an area. You need to learn who are the players, and you need to make partnerships and experiment. It can take ten years of investment before you expect to make any impact whatsoever.

Let me give you one of my favourite examples. It comes out of the work that the *Bridgeway Foundation's* CEO, Shannon Sedgwick Davis has been doing in partnership with an organisation called *Invisible Children*. It works to put an end to the use of child soldiers in the longest running rebel war in central Africa. For over twenty-five years, Joseph Kony has been at the head of the *Lord's Resistance Army* (LRA) a rebel group that has abducted at least 30,000 children in Uganda, the Democratic Republic of Congo, South Sudan, and the Central African Republic. It typically targets kids aged between eight and twelve—they're big enough to carry a gun and young enough to be brainwashed. These kids are told that they must commit atrocities against their own people and if they refuse, they're killed themselves. Some have to kill their own fathers. Then they get taken off to the LRA as porters and soldiers, and the girls as sex slaves. There's no way out because if they try to leave they're killed but even if they do escape they can't go back to their villages.

The Ugandan Government started an amnesty program for these child soldiers, some of whom were now adult, to help them return to their villages. They said that if they came back then they wouldn't be prosecuted by the Government. But how do you get that news to these children? We dropped leaflets from a low-flying Cessna airplane into the war torn areas with the message *My brothers and my sisters come home*. And photos of defectors being welcomed by Ugandan soldiers and embraced by their families. Dropping leaflets from airplanes is not a new idea. But here's something different which I think was a new idea, and for which I must give credit to the people working in Africa. The idea was to go to the villages and record the voices of the mothers calling their sons or daughters back home. Then to play that recording on big loudspeakers from low-flying slow airplanes. It turns out that the voice of a mother is an incredibly powerful force. I think that's brilliant and you don't have to fire a single bullet to make that happen.

How effective was it?

We hired a very expensive firm to come in and evaluate half a dozen things that we tried. Some of them didn't work so well but this one did. On a cost-benefit analysis it's many times more effective and cheaper than using a national army to do this work. The come-home messages can be heard from four miles away and a plane can cover over two hundred square miles in an hour of flying. But I don't want to make out that we're the heroes here. We work with the people who actually get this done. And the real heroes are the ones that come out of the LRA. We have someone working with the *Bridgeway Foundation* who was himself a child soldier. Now he's helping to bring out other child soldiers and to give them employment and a way to reconnect.

Other things we've done include setting up a network of high frequency radios that enable villages to get advance warning of potential attacks from the LRA, and training Ugandan soldiers to track down and capture LRA leaders.

That includes training in human rights and hostage release.

And here's something I learned from the President of Rwanda. He gave a talk last year at the twenty-fifth commemoration of the genocide and said, "There are three steps to forgiveness. You tell the truth, you pay the price and you rejoin the community." It's a brilliant formula. I'm talking to you from Texas where when somebody makes a really bad mistake, we kill them. We execute more people than all but half a dozen entire countries in the world. In Rwanda, one in eight people died and two in eight people were directly complicit. Others, and I'd have to put myself in this category, were bystanders. You can't lock up a third of your country—they had to come up with a different form of justice and the process of figuring out how to rejoin the community is key. If you're serious about that then it's deep and it requires work, and it's worthwhile.

You've described *Bridgeway Capital Management* as a value-driven organisation. What does that mean?

There are a number of things about the culture at *Bridgeway* that come out of thinking about how to live a life. The first thing is to say something about the words we use because they're important. The derivation of the word *employee* is from the French for *to use*. So I tell people, "Don't use that word around me unless you're OK with substituting the words *person being used* for *employee*, and *the user* for *employer.*" It conjures up images of slavery and human trafficking—two things we stand against. There's not a good word in the English language for the relationships that we have here—there are problems with the word *partner* because it implies a partnership form of organisation, which we're not. But it's the best we can come up with and that's what we call everybody who has a full-time commitment to and from *Bridgeway*.

I've talked about our united mission of ending genocide and preventing war atrocities throughout the world. We also have another mission category that we call transformational change and that's basically anything that *Bridgeway* partners want to support. We expect everybody who becomes a partner at *Bridgeway Capital Management* to engage with transformational change somewhere and they get to define what that is. It could be a local shelter for women and children, or homelessness projects, or the environment, for example. Education is a popular area because a number of partners are the first generation in their family to go to college so they've seen how it can transform lives. We put money into a donor advice fund and partners can give it away in any way they want, to support what they're interested in. We have *service days* where we work on projects together in groups and we also have *service trips*. As a firm, we've done four trips to Latin America, digging water wells for potable water. Partners can do a service trip like this with their family—they get a week off and we pay half their expenses. That's one of the most transformative things that we've done. I like borrowing good ideas from other people and that one came from a bank in Tennessee.

Another principle is that partners make a stewardship commitment—in general we pay market wages but at the top end, we've gotten off the track of the outrageous salaries that have become so rampant in corporate America over the last fifty years. We are first and foremost about making a difference for our clients and communities, and this salary practice increases our giving and reduces the need for layoffs in a downturn. And we have a commitment not to do third-party communication at Bridgeway. So if you and I are together and you start complaining about Sally Down The Hall and you say, "I can't believe she did that," I will say, "Hold on a minute. Let's go get Sally." And we'll bring her into the room. We encourage direct conversation and this is between you and Sally—not between you and me. One of the newest members of my team said that although we're much smaller than our most successful competitors, the strengths that they just can't touch are zero politics and no backstabbing. There's power in that because politics and backstabbing are tremendously inefficient.

Where have your influences come from?

My father read philosophy and had an unusual view of capitalism. He was CEO of an oil exploration firm and thought it was a privilege to live in a country where you can start a business, invest and create wealth. He saw that you can do good things for the people that work for you and the people that you serve. Although he was a man of few words, when he said something you listened. He taught me and my siblings that whatever job you do, your life will be richer if you excel at it, treat it with respect and give respect to the people that you work with. It could be a government job...an academic job... digging ditches...or a business job. So I grew up with the thought that you can do good things in the world through business and capitalism, and I still believe that's true. It's not the only way but there are certain efficiencies in business.

I also come from a line of activist women so that's certainly influenced me. My grandmother campaigned for the vote and my mum did a lot of volunteer work. I was the youngest so she'd put me on her hip and take me along with her. She did volunteer work across racial lines in Houston back when that didn't happen much. She just decided it was the right thing to do and was courageous. I remember her being proud of pictures where there's a board of twelve people and she's the only white face in the group.

So I grew up in a home that was intellectually committed. At the dinner table there was a lot of conversation and we played a game called *What If?* My parents would present some situation to me and my three siblings and ask what we'd do. The youngest person had to start first and that was me. I remember being nineteen and the question was *If you suddenly inherited a million dollars what would you do with it?* And I said I would work on the genocide problems in Cambodia.

Relationships are very important to me and I've got some extraordinary support. If you're going to be bold and do risky things then you want to offset that with stability elsewhere in your life. My mother continues to be a support force in my life and I have an amazing spouse. We were twenty-one when we got married and that was forty-two years ago. Statistics on young marriages aren't that good but it worked out great for us. If I'm doing something that's very sad then typically I am very present and solid and strong but she's where I go to recharge. I can let it all out with her. She's an introvert and I'm an extrovert.

One of the wonderful things about philanthropy is learning from people who are doing great stuff. Shannon is on the *Advisory Council of The Elders* and gets to meet people like Jimmy Carter and Archbishop Tutu who work together for peace and human rights. I get copied in on some of the emails and one thing that struck me is how brilliantly Archbishop Tutu expresses appreciation. It made me realise that I have all these appreciative thoughts but I'm busy so I don't actually tell people. Soon after, I was travelling and the plane was delayed. The flight attendant communicated excellently and she also had a difficult passenger to deal with—I thought she handled them brilliantly. I know what good service looks like because at *Bridgeway* we work at it. So later on, she's coming down serving drinks and I say, "Do you have a minute? Can I tell you what I saw?" And she said, "Sure." And I told the story of what I saw her do and she got tears in her eyes. She said, "I've worked here six months and no-one has ever said anything positive to me about what I've done." Six months! This isn't very hard and it doesn't take that much time and it's very powerful. It made me think, "How many missed opportunities have I had in my life? I'm gonna stop doing that."

What do you think are the personal qualities that help you succeed?

I've taken various psychological type tests over the years including the *Myers-Briggs*. One that we use here at *Bridgeway* has been particularly interesting to me as it's pegged how my mind works better than any other instrument. On a metric that they call *vision* I have a very strong score—my mind jumps from thing to thing and I can connect ideas in unusual ways. That's a value that I can add to our investment research team here, or any other random team that you might put me on.

Another thing, like you say in this project, is that everyone has a story or something you can learn from. There's no-one who doesn't have an amazing story if they're willing to own it and tell it to you. So part of my game in life is to find out how to help people open up to tell more of their story. I've got a friend who has talents in cinematography and dance but she says that her superpower is listening—I've tried to adopt that and learn advanced listening skills. Sometimes I find that my time together with people isn't about what it seems to be about. So I try to be open to what's really going on. There are two things I do to create an environment in which people are willing to talk. The first is confidentiality.

The other is non-judgmentalism. That first hit my radar screen about twelve years ago when a book called *UnChristian* came out. It was based on a survey that asked people to take the word *Christianity* and say what three adjectives come to mind. When they did a tally of the top three they were closed-minded, judgmental and homophobic. And when I read that I thought, "Ouch. If that's what it means to be a Christian I hope I'm not one." At this point, I should say that I grew up in a liberal and religious home in the Unitarian denomination, and I identify now as a follower of Jesus—it relates to what's important to me and how I live my life. But one of the things I'm most serious about is not judging other people. In *St. Luke's Gospel* there's a straightforward admonition. It says, "Don't judge or you will be judged by the same standard and we all fall short in some areas." So I really try to practise that.

Have you learned from mistakes?

Definitely. I try to learn from mistakes and not repeat them. One of our traditions at *Bridgeway* is that the newest partner gets given a baseball in a case which they keep till the next partner comes. It says on it *Mistakes are the jewels that allow us to grow and learn*. My biggest professional mistake was in 2004 and it was a miscalculation of how we did fees on performance-based funds at *Bridgeway*. I wrote a four-page letter and put it on our website. In it I said, "As founder of *Bridgeway Funds*, this calculation was absolutely my responsibility, and I am the one at fault." It was my intent to both own what had happened and to communicate with our investors and shareholders. It was also modelling for other people at *Bridgeway* what you do when you screw up, whether small or as here, in a very big way.

And what do you want to do next?

More than half of my close friends have retired but I have no particular thoughts of retiring. I love my work and the people I work with. I feel that if you can work, you work and that's part of making a contribution in the world. It doesn't literally have to mean a job with a pay cheque but it means engaging in something—probably in service to other people.

At sixty-four I'm enjoying my health but I'm not taking it for granted. I'm careful about nutrition and I've run recreationally for most of my life. Last week I ran my fastest ever half-marathon. That's fun and joyful. There's not much I do that I don't find joy in. Genocide and war are horrific and about as dark as it gets but within that process of trying to end it, you can still find moments of joy and celebration—I try to bring those into my life.

I still have half a dozen life goals. One is to celebrate my fiftieth wedding anniversary and another is to run a full marathon at sixty, seventy and eighty years old. I already did sixty. And there's grandparenting, too. I've got eight grandkids ranging from two to college age and I love every one of them. I think I was a little too guarded in raising my kids so I'm wanting to hang out more with my grandkids. I want them to really know who I am and I want to really know them.

Bridgeway Capital Management is on pace but we need to do a lot of work to be the enduring, powerful firm that I think we can be. Another life goal is to give away a hundred million dollars in a year—we've quite some way to go on that yet.

And, we haven't ended genocide yet so that's pretty big...

January 2020

Leonora

"It's very, very interesting to be in late age"

John emails to say that he's thought hard about who to pass me on to. Like several of the recent links, he talked during our interview about the influence that his parent's outlook had on his commitment to social justice. And so it is not a surprise when he chooses his mother as the next link.

He gives me some background information: "My mom is 97 years old, was the first woman PhD in her department at Rice University, got her first full time job in her early sixties when most people are thinking about retiring, did her best professional work at age 94, continues to take courses, swims and does Pilates. Her mind is very sharp—she keeps more up on news than anyone I know. I think she's extraordinary." He ends by asking if it's alright to choose a family member. I say that it is very much alright and that I can't wait to meet her.

Leonora certainly has a very sharp mind. She's also warm and funny. We talk for well over an hour and although I check to make sure that she's not getting tired, she says she's happy to keep going until we've covered the main points. She reflects on her career, and has a lot to say about why we need to change our view of late age. It's fascinating to get some insight from a person who can speak both from an academic perspective and personal experience. This is a woman who cared for her ageing parents, wrote her doctoral thesis on the ethics of old age, and at the age of 95 was delivering sermons with titles such as 'Educating for National Leadership' and 'Fake News, Alternative Facts, Bullshit and the Truth that Sets us Free.'

What did you start out wanting to do?

My parents were both Irish and great raconteurs. Dad was a presidential appointee in the field of aviation and they ran a very hospitable house. There were always interesting people around and I just loved to listen to the adult conversation. Sometimes if I was very quiet and had done my homework I could sit on a little stool and not be sent to bed—they'd forget I was there. Dad's best friend was Russian and he was an international journalist. Whenever he came to visit I was enthralled. He could get into communist Russia when other people couldn't. I read everything he wrote and listened to every radio programme he was on. That's how I decided I was going to be an international journalist.

Now in those days a woman couldn't be married and have a career so my plan was that I would never marry. I remember a high school counsellor talking to me and saying, "But what if you fall in love?" And I said, "I will fight it!"

By the time I got to college, the Second World War had started but the US hadn't yet joined in. The thing I was most concerned about was war and peace. I majored in international politics and I dated Harvard and MIT guys. But I had to let them know they couldn't kiss me because it might lead to falling in love and I couldn't handle that because I was never going to get married!

And how long did that last?

It was during my second year in college that I met this red-headed guy called Jeff from a little town in Texas. He was at Harvard Business School. We were triple dating that night and the guys had to dance with their friends' dates. So I was dancing with him and I said, "What do you plan to do when you leave the Business School?" And he said he wanted to get married and have six sons. Now I never thought of myself as a feminist either then or later but Oh Boy! I stopped dancing and I swelled up and said, "*Sons*? What about daughters?" And he said, "Well as many daughters as come along while I'm having the six sons." I thought, "Some girl is gonna get stuck with this guy." But we fell in love and when I got him down to two boys and two girls, I married him.

He was an extraordinary fellow—just wonderful. He came from a little German settlement of 1500 people in the ranch country of Texas and I was a city girl who'd never been west of the Mississippi. Our backgrounds couldn't have been more different but our family values were the same. It was important to tell the truth, to be kind and to be open-minded. I was just fascinated. He wanted to marry me but he was afraid because he didn't want to marry a career woman. And I realised that if I wanted to live with this man then I had to drop the idea of being an international journalist. It was no sacrifice to me. I was just so thrilled when he asked me to marry him.

Jeff was already qualified as a petroleum engineer and after he left Harvard Business School, he went to law school. The engineering, business and law were a great combination. He had worked in the oil fields as a teenager and was always enthralled with the oil and gas business. We lived in Midland, Fort Worth and Dallas and then finally we moved to Houston. He became CEO of an independent oil company and by then we had four children—two boys and two girls. Although he worked hard, he never brought a briefcase home. He went to the office early and was home for dinner—he was a quiet man who was absolutely devoted to his children and me.

My interests were all about the liberal arts and Jeff became fascinated with this. He started reading philosophy but our personalities were very different. As an engineer, he believed in facts while numbers mean nothing to me and I always ducked math. We often had a guest for dinner and I remember one day I was telling a story and Jeff said to me, "Babe, when you're describing things that have happened, you just ignore zeros." And I was embarrassed as I knew he was right. But I said, "This is not an engineer's report. This is a narrative." He sighed and I went on with my story. That's a pretty good example of how we communicated.

Did you do anything else while you were raising the children?

I saw my career as parenting and in those days you had to be home when the kids came back from school at three o'clock. If you weren't then you were seen as a bad mother or a lazy mother. And I was really interested in my kids—each one was different. Jeff and I had the philosophy of letting them suffer the consequences when they stumbled and not picking them up unless they were in danger. In my day that was good parenting. I remember being very influenced by a book called *Logical Consequences for Parents*. It's different today.

I had time while the kids were at school, though, and I became involved in volunteer work in the community. It had occurred to me that all the things I had pondered about solving the problems of war, could be applied to a city instead of the world. I thought that you could solve poverty problems if you just had a good plan for the whole city. So when somebody asked me to serve on the board of a non-profit organisation I agreed. And the thing is that if you read the reports and you show up for meetings, they'll ask you on another board and so pretty soon I was involved in a lot of boards. This included being President of the Day Care Association and chair of the Drug Abuse Council.

How much success do you feel you had?

There are two that I'm particularly proud of. One was the Parents' League which we started from scratch. This was to stop the *too much, too soon* social pattern for children. About 4500 families in Southwest Houston were involved and we proved that you can change the culture. We were very democratic about it. I chaired the committee that got driver's licensing moved from age fourteen to sixteen through state legislation. People said it couldn't be done but we did it.

The other one was being on the community welfare planning board for the United Way in Houston. Instead of having a number of different organisations all working separately, this was a way for them to pool their fundraising and support efforts and to look at the whole community. This was what I was dying to do—to look at the whole community. It got very political and I was right in the middle of that. The Fifth Ward neighbourhood had a lot of poverty problems and a lot of bad stuff went on there—people felt unsafe. We wanted to address some of these problems but we thought it was important to find out what the people there felt they needed. That's kind of different from finding out what people are doing. I was chair of that group with three staff. Every Wednesday night for about thirteen weeks, we got a car and went into the Ward. Looking back, my husband must have been quite concerned but he was always supportive. I got really well acquainted with the leaders in the community and that was an education for me. I have a photo of the group I worked with and I'm the only white person in the picture. I love that picture. I loved those people.

But after I'd been working in the community for some time I felt that I was getting nowhere. Jeff said to me, "You know Babe, you've been working at this for fifteen years and sometimes it seems like putting your fist in a marshmallow—you take it out and it goes right back where it was." That was hard to hear and I wished he hadn't said it but I began to really doubt that what I'd hoped for, was possible. It made me feel that I still didn't know enough, so I gradually got off the boards and I started doing some courses in sociology at Rice University. I was looking for answers to questions but what I found was that they didn't know as much as we did in the community. Then I stumbled into a religion course almost by fluke.

I'm a Unitarian Universalist and that's how Jeff and I raised the children. But I'd just done the usual church things and hadn't paid a lot of attention. Then I began to study religious ethics and found I loved it. It helped me with that question I was always after. *What should we be doing?* I learned how to think about self in relation to community and that helped as I guess I was never satisfied that I had a handle on what I was aiming at. You can put yourself at the centre of a series of concentric circles. And you can think about what skills and strengths you have, what powers, and what your health is like. Then outside of yourself is the circle of your immediate family. If you go a little broader that's your neighborhood, and beyond that are the circles for your city and then your state and then your nation and pretty soon it's the world. Now, sometimes all of the good things that people do are with that first concentric circle of family, and then there are people like Desmond Tutu who give to the broadest circle, for all of us, thank God.

John said that you come from a family of strong women. How do you think that influenced you?

Well, my grandmother died when I was a year old so I never knew her. But when I was an adult I was given her daytimer by a cousin. And when I opened it, there was my story, the same as hers. Half of her appointments were family, and half were community. She lived in Anderson, Indiana, and was never a suffragette but she marched with them to get the vote. She was active in her church, and she organised the Current Events club where people could discuss social and political events. And she was on the first library board in the town. This was one of the Carnegie libraries—imagine, libraries in every little town, one of the most underrated gifts that was ever given in this country. Her name was Leonora and that's my middle name—my first name is Rachel but when she died it was a terrible blow to my mother and they started calling me Leonora.

My mother was very close to my grandmother and lived just two doors down the street. Mother was pretty in the style of her day, and the most popular girl in town. She rode the fastest horse and she drove a car from the very beginning. She was always game for things. And she was the best mother-in-law you could ever be. She was wise and generous-spirited. When my brother and I both moved away she never said, "Oh gosh, this is going to be hard on me." Instead she said, "Honey, goodbye. You're going to have a wonderful life."

We were very close and some years later when she had a

stroke, Jeff and I moved her from Washington to Houston. She was blind and we had her at home for about six months. She went into a real serious depression. We tried everything and nothing worked. She couldn't eat or sleep and I was beside myself. One thing led to another and in the end the only thing left to try was shock treatment. First of all, I said I would never agree to that but we felt we had to do something. My Dad and brother and I talked about it with the doctor and he said that she might not survive the treatment but in the end we all agreed that she was in so much mental pain that we were willing to risk it. She had three treatments and after that she wasn't in pain any more but she was memory-impaired. She knew that I belonged to her but she couldn't say my name. By then she needed nursing-home care and we moved her several times. It was three and a half years before she died. We knew we were going to lose her and it was a sad time, a heavy time. Then my Dad moved in with us for the last five years of his life, and he died at home.

I was interested in the topic of old age as I'd seen my mother and Dad through the end of their lives. And I enrolled to do a doctorate at Rice University. It was about the ethics of old age—what people can do with the powers that remain despite disintegration and limitation, and the theological view of this. The end of our lives is a *big deal* and can make or break the worth of our whole life. If we were to develop more of an awareness of this there would be quite a social change. It would mean doing what we could so that people had everything possible going for them in old age.

What happened as the kids grew up and you had more time?

Jeff had a heart attack when he was in his early fifties. He did everything he could to prolong his life for the next ten years but he knew he was going to die. I couldn't bear to think about losing him so I didn't even try. But finally, one time we were in the kitchen and I said to him, "You don't think you're going to live very long do you?" He just said very quietly, "No I don't." I remember that moment so clearly. And of course you're never ready. When he did die, he was sixty-two and I was fifty-nine. My father died five weeks after Jeff.

I finished my doctorate and I knew that I needed to do something with my life. I was young enough, I was healthy, my kids were raised, I had enough money, and I was educated. I'd had a wonderful husband and a great family life and so I was fortunate. By that time I had nine grandchildren in Houston and I was scared to death that I'd be overpresent to my children. The only time I felt happy was when I was with them but they didn't need me there that much.

Some of Jeff's friends came to me and said, "You could do this—and you could do that—" So I narrowed it down to a couple of things. I hadn't had a job at all since six months after we were married and I thought perhaps I could be an executive secretary for some CEO. After all I'd been a businessman's wife. Or I could think about training for the ministry.

And what did you do?

A year later I was ordained as a Unitarian Universalist minister. I was an associate at my church for a few years and then I started looking for a new church where I could be a minister. I applied for three and there were a couple of disappointments but in 1989 when I was sixty-six, I was called as full-time minister to a church. They decided they wanted to move so they bought land and built a new church. I was an absolute novice. I didn't know how to grow a church but we had a great time together and I was there for seven years.

I've also done some work in Europe and every year for about ten years I would go over and take services at English-speaking fellowships in Belgium, France, Germany and the Netherlands. I was there so often they thought I was their minister! That was a treat.

You've lived a long life, Leonora. What do you think has got better in your lifetime, and what's got worse?

What has gotten better...? Maybe that the political and cultural discourse has spread through the whole country. Young people like my grandchildren get all their information digitally. I think they might find a way to save our democracy. But I have to keep asking myself how we got in this dilemma. I grew up in Washington and went to the White House several times. I met three presidents—Hoover, Roosevelt and Truman, and the Oval Office is sacred ground for me. Clinton disappointed me badly—maybe I could have handled what he did if it happened across the street at Blair House but that he acted like that in the Oval Office with such contempt. That scandalised me. I was very shaken up about Nixon, too, but we knew what to do about it and we got rid of him.

I am sure that every president that walks into that office for the first time must be thunderstruck by the responsibility. But Ye Gods! They are stepping into a unique and super powerful job so how could it happen that the majority of the electorate put Trump there? It's not what people said about him, it's what he showed us on television. We can all see it—and I have intelligent friends who voted for him. They say, "Well Leonora, we don't like the way he talks but he's done good things." I say, "He stumbles into something on Monday and on Wednesday he changes his mind. Don't you see it?" But that's fake news. And you just can't win. I could go on and on. Our system that was set up by the Founding Fathers, I thought it was the salvation of the planet but for the first time in my life I don't have that confidence. It's very weighty with me.

How does it feel to be in your late nineties?

People often say to me, "I want to be like you when I'm old, Leonora." The thing is that they see me at my best because I come alive with people, but if they saw me for the first fifteen minutes after I get out of bed in the morning, they wouldn't want it. I'm slower and some parts of my mind are slower. The other thing is that I'm being rapidly left behind because I don't know the language of the digital world. I use a computer and send emails but I lose them and am not wise in this method of communication. That's a problem because I am a communicator.

It's very, very interesting to be in late age. Our culture tells us that after eighty-five, we're just *elderly*. But it's not like that at all. The difference between being ninety-four and ninety-seven is quite remarkable. There's a whole load of us ninety-somethings but there's very little literature on it. I know a lot about late age and I'm fascinated by it. You see the world differently, and I keep changing my understanding of it. There must be other people out there feeling the same, and they ought to be heard. But who's going to be interested if you're not there yet? People suggest I write it down but these days I'm subject to some confusion. My comments would be scattered. There's too much going on in my head. Some days it's spinning with eight unrelated topics.

My grandchildren are very important to me. I've got twelve now and they're fascinating. I love spending time with them and about ten years before the turn of the century we started planning a weekend together, so that we could celebrate the new millennium. One day I had five of them in the back of the car and we were talking about it. *Should we be on a mountain top, or should we be by the sea?* Finally I said, "I'll tell you what I think." And James who was seven said, "Granny it doesn't matter what you think. You're gonna be dead." Now, I'm proud to report that there was uproar in the rest of the car and they all said, "James! *Don't* say that." So to save James from being thrown out of the car I said, "I will live well past the turn of the century because I'm going to live to be a hundred." So from then on everyone has believed absolutely that I am going to live to be a hundred. Then I thought that I don't want to die on my hundredth birthday so I added a year and said, "I will live to be a hundred and one."

And you know, I probably will. But I *am* closing in on it!

February 2020

Tim

"Doing things that people say you can't do, gets attention"

With typical efficiency Leonora has arranged a prompt handover. But in the few weeks since we spoke, the coronavirus pandemic has changed the world and almost everything about everyday life is odd at the moment.

I'm going to be speaking to Tim. Leonora is best friends with his mother and has known him since he was tiny. She tells me that he is inventive and that through him she learned that a formal education can sometimes be limiting rather than liberating. She adds that "his resume is unique—or it would be if he ever slowed down enough to write one!"

Tim lives in California where he runs a vineyard. He agrees to do a video call and asks his executive assistant Erin to arrange it. We have several email exchanges and of course can't fail to mention the pandemic. Erin replies to one email with "Things are very strange here as well. We are also under orders to 'shelter in place' in our homes. Trying to navigate these new circumstances. Every day is a new adventure and we're just trying to keep up!" Stay safe, is a standard sign-off for everyone these days.

Tim has achieved much in his life, largely through finding innovative ways to do things that other people say are impossible. He became known throughout the United States for rescuing gigantic old trees and replanting them elsewhere. Many experts had said this couldn't be done and it's certainly a problem that I've never thought about before. But it's always interesting to learn unexpected things through these interviews. Tim explains the procedure to me, in layman's terms and by the end of our conversation, I am very pleased to have a rough understanding of how to re-locate a giant tree.

What's life like for you at the moment, Tim?

I live in an amazing spot in California. We're about an hour and a half north of the Golden Gate Bridge, and I'm in charge of day-to-day operations at the winery I bought with my brother in 2004. It's a tough, competitive industry—the big guys really control the market so we try to give ourselves an edge by being sustainable. It keeps us relevant but to be honest, the main reason I'm interested in sustainability is that my parents raised me to believe you should leave things better than you find them. A lot of people think it costs more to be sustainable but it really doesn't. It's about being efficient and that has an impact environmentally, economically and emotionally. I make decisions based on data. So, for example, I no longer irrigate automatically on particular days. I measure the moisture three feet down in the ground and only water when my data tells me to.

Is that unusual in the wine industry?

It's still not terribly common, but as water becomes a critical issue it's increasing. Here in California, it's not just a matter of whether you have enough money to buy water—there might not be water to buy. So it's important to be efficient by doing things like reducing irrigation and recycling waste water. Our facility is quite large and the buildings alone take up about six acres. I used to have one water meter feeding the entire facility but that meant I couldn't figure out where all the water was being used. So I put in twenty-two separate water meters and the first thing I found was a leak under a building that had probably been there for about twenty years. So we fixed that. Then a couple of months later I was walking through the barrel room and one of the workers stopped me. He's been there for twenty-eight years and said, "Tim, I see you put a meter right here on my building. You're gonna know how much water I'm wasting, aren't you?" And I said, "No. I'm gonna know how much water you're saving." All of a sudden he's being measured for something positive, and now those twenty-five guys up there are all competing to see who can use the least water.

About five years ago when we were having a very bad drought, the State Water Resources Control Board showed up and asked us to reduce our water usage by thirty-five per cent. I pulled out all my data and showed them that I'd already reduced it by fifty per cent. They said, "Oh never mind. You're fine. Can you show your neighbours how to do this."

Leonora said that you're a problem solver. Where does that come from?

I remember being about six years old, and somebody saying to me, "Get down from there! You can't do *that*." And I learned right then that *can't* might mean *shouldn't* but it doesn't mean *couldn't*. So I proceeded to do things that people said you weren't supposed to do. When I was about thirteen my friend and I figured out how to break into a shopping centre, and I used to *borrow* cars, though I always put them back. I was bored and these things were a challenge. Doing things that people say you can't do, gets attention, and when I started work I learned that solving problems means you get to charge more money.

What was your first job?

My parents had already told me and my siblings that they did not believe in inherited wealth, and school wasn't working out well for me so I decided not to waste time on it. I finished at the age of fifteen and went to work on ranches where people didn't care how old I was or whether I was in school. I did that till I was seventeen at which point I was able to buy a pick-up truck and start a small landscape company—mowing people's lawns and things like that.

I built that up pretty quickly and started doing commercial projects. During the 1970s we opened offices in Houston, Austin, Dallas, and San Antonio and had about fifty workers in each. In the 1980s we spread out to Las Vegas, Orlando, and Atlanta. Most of my work in Orlando was for Walt Disney World. Through that we also got the work at Euro Disney and so we had an office in Paris. By then we had around five hundred people working for us.

You became known across the US for moving enormous old trees. How did that happen?

It was when I was landscaping big, expensive properties. Often they'd ask me to cut down trees because they were in the way of the new buildings, and so we started rescuing them. It's common practice to transplant small trees with trunks about four inches in diameter. But if you get up to twelve inches and more, then it almost never happens. When I'd suggest moving a big tree my clients would line up consultants with PhDs and they'd say, "You can't move that tree. It's not gonna work." I'd ask them why I couldn't move it and when they told me, I would usually figure out a way to do it.

So, for instance I was working on a resort hotel at Walt Disney World and we had to build an island in the middle of a lagoon. The architect sent over a model, and in the middle by a swimming pool was a big tree. The branches came down and almost touched the pool and they were asking me to construct it out of concrete and fibre glass. When they told me what the budget was, I said, "Wouldn't you rather have a real living tree?" Their answer was, "Tim, you know this is fifty feet across." I asked for a couple of days to think and talked to a friend who worked for Disney and had maps showing all the future projects. Walt Disney World is a very large piece of property—about 26,000 acres including a lot of old farms. We got in a helicopter and found two oaks in an area that was going to become the All-Star Hotel. They were over two hundred years old with great big branches that swung down and touched the ground. Exactly like what they wanted me to build out of concrete. I convinced them to let me move *both* trees as it was going to cost a couple of hundred thousand dollars to move one including closing a freeway, and so I could move the second one almost for free. That got plenty of attention and as people started realising that it could be done, I got phone calls from all over the country. A hospital down in Florida wanted to put up an additional building but there were two old oaks in the way, and the community wouldn't agree to cut them down. So the hospital called me and we moved one tree a hundred feet in this direction and the other a hundred feet in that direction. They got to build their hospital and the neighborhood got to keep their big, old trees.

How did you figure out how to move such big trees?

When we start talking about a project, I pull people together for a meeting and tell them that we're going to be there for thirty minutes. We'll spend the first fifteen minutes talking about solutions and how we can get this job done. If people have reasons to think we can't get it done then I tell them to write them down and we'll deal with those in the second fifteen minutes. Change is difficult for a lot of people and I figured out a long time ago that if you allow the meeting to start with reasons you *can't* get things done, then everything takes a whole lot longer. What usually happens in these meetings is that people see each other coming up with solutions and want to be part of the team that's making things happen. Then they start coming up with their own solutions and so the second fifteen minutes is usually more like five minutes.

When it comes to actually moving big trees then you follow the same principles as moving a small tree. You cut down into the ground and pick up the root ball. But the thing is that the root ball might be the size of a small back yard. And it might weigh five hundred tons so you can't pick the tree up by the trunk—you have to put something underneath the root ball to support it. It's like a cake sitting on the dining room table. If you wanted to move it, you couldn't just pick it up. It would fall apart in your hands. So we dig a large flat pit off to the side, maybe sixty feet by eighty feet and as deep as the root ball goes. We lay big steel pipes across the pit, sometimes as many as forty. Then we use a big hammer—the sort you use to break concrete—to drive each pipe across horizontally until it's under the root ball. What we end up with is this great round ball of dirt sitting on the ground with pipes sticking out of each side like a cake sitting on a grill. We hook the pipes onto steel beams and use hydraulic jacks to raise everything up and lift it onto something that can roll. For the really big ones I've used trailers with 118 wheels. We retain moisture in the root ball by covering it with burlap, hog wire and surround wrap. When we've moved the tree to where we want it, we do everything in reverse. We lift it up with jacks, pull the trailer out, and set the tree in its new position. The pipes stay with the tree.

Every time we moved a tree we'd go bigger and bigger. The largest was a sycamore with a trunk that was seventy-six inches across with a circumference of almost three hundred inches. It's the obstacles between point A and point B, like bridges, that limit the size of what you can move.

The question people always ask is, "Won't that tree die?" And my answer is, "Oh, absolutely. But probably not in my lifetime." All trees die eventually but often when people think they can't be moved it's because they don't understand the aftercare. It has to be sufficient. So, for example, there was a problem with one of the Walt Disney World trees about six years after we moved it. A lot of the leaves turned yellow and fell off, so the management got me and a couple of consultants to go and look at it. One of them thought it was caused by ozone, another that it was the chlorine in the swimming pool and the other thought it had been struck by lightning. I could see that the ground was moist so I knew the tree was getting water. But I didn't see the girl whose responsibility it was to take care of the tree. When I asked the gardeners, they said she'd been transferred to Epcot and there was now a new manager who didn't think anyone should be personally responsible for the tree. I worked out that they'd stopped watering but had turned it back on when the leaves started falling off. Pretty shortly that tree completely turned around and was fine.

How does it feel when you see those trees in their new place?

It's a great feeling. Some of these trees were there when George Washington was around, or even when Christopher Columbus landed, and we've saved them. One of the differences between landscaping and construction is that the day you finish a building, that's as good as it's ever going to look. With landscaping, the day you finish is just the beginning and if done properly that landscape will look even better twenty years on.

So you had a very successful landscaping business. What happened next?

Somebody came along and convinced me to stop doing work for other people and just do projects for him. He was an extremely wealthy individual and he was also brilliant. There were things he wanted to do that he knew would be challenging for most people to wrap their heads around, but he'd seen a video of us moving those trees and he realised that I don't believe in *can't*. It took three days for him to convince me to go and work for him. I'd defied many things and despite not going to school and being young, I'd been quite successful and had the greatest clients in the world. His answer was that I'd only been preparing for my work with him. And he was right. I became his right hand and lived with him on and off for eleven years. He was extremely demanding and kept everyone away. I was one of the only people that got anywhere near him. We spent the 1990s building the three largest privately-held indigenous botanical gardens in the US—in New York, South Florida and Aspen, Colorado.

How did you get from that to owning a winery?

It was around 1999 that I started thinking about what I would regret not doing and I just kept coming back to the same two things. I wanted to live somewhere similar to paradise. And I wanted as much of my family around me as possible because for many years I only saw my parents, siblings, nieces and nephews once or twice a year if somebody died or got married. That was not sufficient for me. I'd got the botanical gardens to the point where they didn't need me anymore, although that could have been a job for life if I'd wanted it. So I spent three years looking round the country for the right property. I looked at over three hundred in places like Florida Keys, Central Texas and New Mexico. I ended up here in California—it's an interesting climate. In July it might be a hundred degrees during the day so you can swim, and then forty-five degrees at night so you can have a fireplace. I like both those things.

When I first started looking, I called my parents and said, "I'm gonna figure out where I want to live for the rest of my life. And I want you to come too." They laughed and said they couldn't do that. I told them that if they were going to stay in Houston for the rest of their lives then they'd only see me once or twice a year, and I wouldn't know the people taking care of them. They were about seventy at the time and when they got off the phone, they started looking round at their friends, many of whom were about ten years older. And they saw how things would be. They called me back and said, "How's the search going?"

Within a few months of me coming here, my parents moved. They're in a nice, safe spot about fifteen minutes away and they have everything they need. I see them a couple of times a week and I cannot imagine what it would be like if they were still in Houston. One of my older children showed up, too, and I now have about fifteen family members all within an hour—my brother and his wife, nieces and nephews—and my sister and her husband come visit from North Carolina. Most weekends we have between fifteen and thirty people at the home ranch.

And what next?

I'm now sixty-four so I'm only a year or two from retirement which is just fine with me and I'm watching my nephew take the reins of the company. I'm divorced but in a relationship and I've got two dogs. There are plenty of things I like to do but I really have achieved my goals. When we first came here, I had a bad virus and a spinal tap that went wrong. I had the worst headache you can imagine. For about three days I lay there thinking I was dying—and I realised then that I was content with what I'd accomplished. I live in a beautiful place and I have my family around me.

March 2020

Spencer

"I like to give objects a new life in a way that makes people marvel at the materials or wonder what they were originally"

Tim passes me on to his friend Spencer and tells me that he is an accomplished musician and 'a pillar of our community.' They've known one another for many years and worked together at the winery for a while. Tim says he is sure that I will find Spencer's story very interesting.

Despite being over five thousand miles apart, Spencer and I are in similar circumstances at the moment—restrictions due to the coronavirus pandemic. There's not much to celebrate about the current global situation but at least with no one getting out much, I'm able to fix up these interviews with fewer delays.

I email Spencer and he replies promptly and positively saying, "I am honored I somehow got passed your way. Love the concept of your book, should be an interesting journey across many lives and disciplines." It seems a bit repetitive and undiscerning somehow, to keep saying that the interviewees are warm, open and friendly. But the fact is that they all are, *and of course that is to be expected as it's precisely these characteristics that make them appealing to other people.*

Spencer sends me links to three websites that give me a clue to the important things in his life—his music, his sculptures, and the home that he shares with his wife Esther and regular paying guests. I read that guests sleep in a converted recording studio where Spencer produced hundreds of records and made seventeen solo albums. They can have a private concert from Spencer, go horse-riding in the Northern Californian countryside or just spend time sitting in the garden. The pictures show a huge chessboard with alternating squares of turf and paving slabs. There are sculpted figures on some of the squares—Alice, the Mad Hatter and the White Rabbit. A Cheshire Cat lounges on a nearby water feature and

I spot a quirky table and chairs. Here at the nineteenth link in the chain I seem to have gone full circle back to Kirsti's Alice in Wonderland themed table. But I'm not quite finished yet. I've decided that twenty is a nice round number at which to stop so I still have Spencer's story to hear, and then there is the question of where he will send me next.

Tell me about the place where you live, Spencer...

Mendocino County is two hours north of San Francisco. It's the size of Scotland but it's very remote and the population is only about 88,000. We've got mountains, and it's where the gigantic redwood trees meet the vineyards of Northern California. It's a beautiful place with clean air, no traffic, and great water. Over time we found out it was the most liberal county in the nation. Esther has horses and over the past thirty-five years we've bought a few extra acres. We built a recording studio in the nineties and made over three hundred albums, some film scores, radio commercials, and high-tech messaging industry content here. We've also fostered about a hundred kids, mostly emergency foster care.

We feel very lucky to have got here when we did but I am originally from Texas—the sixth generation. I'm the escaped Texan or as my family say, 'the black rainbow'—the first and only member of my family to leave Dallas.

Can we go back to the beginning. How did Texas influence you?

My father was an insurance businessman and I guess we were a typical 1950s family. We lived in North Dallas and as a kid I just took for granted what we had around us. In my town we had Texas Instruments where calculators were invented, Collins Radio which built satellite communications for the space race, and the University of Texas research centres. There were ham radio antennae all over people's houses and there was a PhD in roughly every seventh household. My oldest friend Ricky lived down the street and his Dad had three PhDs. I was told that he was one of only three people in the world who by using weather predictions could predict where and when spacecraft would splashdown. The other two were Russian. He had maps all over the house and would be looking at them for months before a space mission took off.

I remember one day, I must have been about eleven and I'm playing with Ricky when his Dad comes up and says, "Hey boys, I'm going in to work. Do you wanna come along and see something interesting?" So, we say, "Sure," and he takes us out to this big warehouse. We go past a couple of Army sentries and eventually we come to this room, the size of a gymnasium. Ricky's dad says, "Now boys, I've got to do some work. You stay in there—it's a lot of fun but don't touch anything." So we walk in and there are these great, long tables with a load of rocks on them. We're just kids and we're looking at these things and we're thinking, "What's the big deal? They're just rocks." There are a couple of sentries there so we go up to one and ask what's going on. And that's when we find out that the whole room's filled with moon rocks. Wow, we're blown out by that. Then we go over to another table and there are these photographs unlike anything we've ever seen before. They're crystal clear and look like they're from another planet, and of course they are. Ricky's dad told us later, "That's something we're experimenting with. It's called *digital* and we're working on it with NASA. No-one knows about it yet." Of course that meant nothing to us and then if I remember correctly, as we went out Ricky slipped one of the really little rocks into his pocket. Then we went home and played in the creek—I think we lost the rock.

Another friend's dad was on a team of six people and when I asked him what they did he said, "We go in a room and we think. One day we thought up the calculator. And another day we invented the cassette deck." These were the kind of people I hung out with and it helped to shape me because I thought everything was possible.

How did you get into music?

That began with an old upright piano that my mother and grandmothers bought for my Dad. He'd always said, "You wanna be a hit at a party? Then play the piano." But when we got it, he never had the time to play, so I started and my mother sent me to piano lessons. I hated them. My first recital piece was Beethoven's Für Elise, like all kids, and I practised for nine months. I had it nailed down and then on the day of the recital, I forgot the entire middle part and ran off stage crying. I convinced my Mom to let me stop taking lessons but in her wisdom she said I still had to play for an hour a day.

The thing that really opened the door for me, was playing music with my grandmother. Her name was Alma Lovelace Gertrude Brewer but we all called her Doody. She was quite a character—a Southern belle with a blonde beehive, a long cigarette holder, and a gin and tonic on the piano. She treated me like I was something special because she felt I was her reincarnated husband. Of course, as a kid I didn't know any of this. I'd be playing with my toys on the floor and she'd say in her thick southern accent, "Speeanca, you come over here, baby. You sit right next to your ol' Doody. C'mon sweetheart, you sit right here and I'm gonna teach you how to play boojie woojie music." She taught me to play the blues. "Oh my God!" I thought, "I can play something that's fun and outrageous and not on a piece of sheet music." So I started experimenting and wrote my first song when I was eleven or twelve. I didn't think anything of it but over the years realised that I had the gift of melody. I'm not saying that as an ego thing—it's just that I could hear melodies in my head and write songs in minutes. It was like a fever and it made me see myself as different and special. I was young and I had an obnoxious, Texan attitude to boot. It took a long time for that attitude to get knocked out of me.

How did you get into the music business?

After I left high school I moved to Austin, Texas to find my hippy self. I wanted to be a rock and roll musician so I played piano at night, and during the day I'd wait for the phone to ring because that's what drug dealers do. Then I met a guy named Billy Ray McCauley who was larger than life and looked like Santa Claus in flowing scarves. He'd written this book called *Once Upon a Time* which was a campy version of *Cinderella* and we started working together to develop a musical of it.

I worked on the Mississippi Queen steamboat on and off at that time, and on one cruise I was waiter to a guy named Tom. All week I recited poems to him and his entourage and he and his family would applaud at each meal. On the last night I told him they were the lyrics for this musical and he got me to go to the empty ball room and play grand piano for him and his wife. It was like, one in the morning and most of the ship was asleep. For over two hours I recited every line and sang every character, and at the end he said, "What are you doing on this boat?" He handed me five hundred dollars which was a lot of money for me in those days and said, "You get off this boat and I'll come and pick you up in my private jet. We're gonna find out what to do with you." It was like a film. And sure enough, he flew to Fulton, Missouri and took me by private jet and Rolls Royce to his office in Indianapolis.

Then he got the biggest producer in the city to listen and see if he thought there was anything there. They decided that they wanted to produce the musical and paid for me and Billy Ray to live in The Hamptons while we worked on it. We did that for a long time, going up to New York to watch musicals and then coming back and rewriting. But in the end I just couldn't be with Billy Ray anymore. It was getting too intense so I walked away, and that's what really started my music career. When I took out the lyrics to the songs, I was left with very melodic music and the New Age music movement was just taking off at that time. It was all about minimalist but high-quality production with no vocals. We hated the designation *New Age Music*, but that's what stuck. So I started a record company and put out my first album, *Where Angels Dance*. I rode the wave on that movement with a number of artists on my label and around fifty distributors. But eventually I realised I was spending ninety per cent of my time running the business and only about ten per cent on the music, so I sold it along with the rights to my next seven records, to one of my distributors—Narada, a large New Age label.

Another thing I did was to put on music events. That started right back in North Dallas with a guy called Ron Kinnamon who ran the YMCA in our town. As a teenager I spent a lot of time helping him with things like landscaping the new Y, coaching, canoe guiding, and magic classes. Then he started running Indian Guide camps for a couple of hundred fathers and daughters in Texas and Oklahoma. There'd be just one or two of us helping, and the idea was for the fathers and daughters to have fun and get to understand one another better. There was always something big at the end so I got plenty of experience of putting on events with a lot of infrastructure. I did this with Ron for years and we also wrote the national YMCA theme song together. They still sing that round campfires today. Ron eventually became second in charge of the YMCA of the USA. He was my hero early on—the father I wanted to have.

My work with the YMCA led to me becoming a musical ambassador for Big Brothers Big Sisters of America when I was on Narada. That's a big youth mentoring charity here in the States. I spent five years touring the US on and off, and performing with people like football stars and actors, in front of thousands. It was about raising money for the charity but also educating them how to do these kinds of events.

Why do you say that was Ron the father you wanted to have?

My father loved me a great deal but he didn't quite understand me. I come from several generations of college graduates and he expected me to carry on that tradition. I was supposed to be a businessman but here I was, a rock and roll musician with long hair. Ron understood that but my dad and grandfather fought it a lot.

That did eventually change when I became a little famous round the country. There were three radio stations in Dallas that played my music constantly and I had the same name as my dad. He'd get asked in airports and restaurants, "Are you *that* Spencer Brewer?" The point at which he accepted me was when the *Dallas Morning News* did an article and took a photo of him standing next to a poster of me. He was quite proud from then on.

You mentioned earlier that you've done fostering...

Esther and I spent twenty-plus years as emergency foster care parents and because she's a marriage and family therapist we had some of the more difficult cases. That changed both of us and it was an extremely rich and humbling experience, learning about those kids' lives. They were all in some kind of crisis.

I guess the most important thing we were able to offer was a safe place in a world where they didn't feel safe. And they had permission to say things that perhaps they couldn't normally say without getting hit. We offered whatever each particular kid needed, whether that was solitude, or having a conversation with an adult that wasn't full of anger and yelling. Some had never eaten at a dinner table in their life. They'd only seen it on TV. We were able to give them that experience. A couple of them became our long-term foster kids and now we're foster grandparents to their kids.

How did things go with the music?

Things changed in a couple of ways. Firstly, I had a car accident in 1999. It was a head-on collision and I lost around eighty per cent of my long-term memory, and my short-term memory was affected too. Before that, I could hear melodies all the time. It was like I had a radio channel in my head and whatever we needed for a production, in whatever genre, it was there. But after I was in that car wreck, the radio channel turned off and things shifted. I still played concerts but I no longer had non-stop musical creativity. That never came back. Instead of writing two songs a week, I might write two songs a year. The other thing was that the music industry collapsed in 2008 and I lost four companies all based around the music industry.

Tell me about your sculptures...

I never could have predicted that I'd shift my creative focus from music into a physical form like sculptures. But it was somewhat of an easy transition because I've worked with my hands all my life. It feels like all of that experience with rebuilding and repairing pianos has given my hands memory and wisdom so they have their own way of finding solutions. That may sound strange about hands having their own memory or ability but it *is* how I experience it.

My sculptures are made mainly from mechanical objects that were crafted in the period between the early 1800s and the 1920s. They fascinate me because that was an era when people had access to more quality materials than they'd ever had before and there was a focus and diligence around craftsmanship rather than mass production. I found a perfect example of that in a big, old clock I took apart. It was made around 1850 and deep inside the recess was a part that had beautiful scrollwork on it. Someone had gone to all the trouble of making it like that, then they'd put it inside the clock where no-one would ever see it. What was all that about? Then one of my compatriots gave me the perfect answer—"No-one else will see it, but the person who made it will know, and God will know." That makes sense to me though I'm not talking about a religious god. For me it's more about the big picture. If I build something then I want to do it to the best of my ability.

So I seek out objects from that era that are made of exceptional materials and I love to know their provenance. I don't paint them, heat them or change them other than making them into sculptures. I like to give them new life in a way that makes people marvel at the materials or wonder what they were originally. Some pieces come together real quick, and others need patience and take months or even years. Like my sculpture, Tesla Man. That took two years and was inspired by the life of Nikola Tesla. I wanted to honour him because he was a great genius and came up with all kinds of electrical inventions like alternating current, induction motors, neon bulbs, vacuum tubes, radio, and Tesla coils, but his genius was centuries ahead of his era and he died alone and broke in a New York hotel room.

I started with a male mannequin that I'd bought for five bucks when a department store went out of business. It had been in my workshop for a long time and I wasn't sure what to do with it till I decided to use it for this sculpture. It was six foot one, and muscular but the right arm and head were missing. I started looking for clothes and objects from Nikola Tesla's era and I found a prosthetic arm that was made in World War One in Croatia. That's where he was born, and then I found an old plasma globe for him to hold, and a violet wand—both electrical items that he invented. That took months. And in the meantime, I'd contacted Dick Billups who's a local electrical genius and asked him to build a Tesla coil as the mannequin's head. He also manufactured a whole lot of electronics that went inside the body cavity.

There are so many parts to this thing. The top of the podium is made out of a German piano from the 1880s, the base uses English organ pipes from the 1890s, and there are porcelain knife light switches from the turn of the century. The wiring in his legs are made of knob and tube insulators from an 1890s house. When you switch him on, the plasma globe and violet wands light up and 7,500 Volts go through him like lightning. The sparks are very loud. He's only been out of here three times and that's been when I've taken him to art shows. Each time, he's won an award and gotten a lot of attention. Growing up around so many electrical professionals I guess I came full circle with Tesla Man.

What does creativity mean to you?

I think it's about giving yourself permission to be raw and to make mistakes. I imagine it like putting your hand on a door—you don't know yet what's on the other side and that can be scary because the minute you open the door there might be a dozen...or a hundred...or thousands of people looking at you. But I've learned to trust that whatever shows up will be OK. The creativity is there. You just have to let go and allow it to come out.

I believe that everybody has a creative talent but many people find it hard to work out what theirs is. That creativity may get sparked early on, or it may happen later in life. It doesn't matter what it is, the important thing is that it matters to you and that you get joy out of it. Mine happened to look big and was in front of other people on stage, but it could be knitting or something else you do by yourself. We need to allow ourselves to find that talent and give ourselves permission to do it without being judged by anyone else.

Around the art, Esther and I encourage people to come to our studio and build their own stuff and I remember one woman in particular. She comes in one day and says, "I don't do art... I love it... I collect it... but I don't *do* it." And I say, "Right, here's something anybody can do. Have a look at the shelves and pick out some things that appeal to you...maybe that doll's head...or that watch. Then sit them on the table," and I walk away. So she does that and I ask if she sees these things being on a wall or on a table. "On a wall," she says. Then I ask what shape frame she sees them in—square, round, triangular... And she says, "Square." That's just a little bit of time and she's got all this stuff on the table that appeals to her, and she knows that she likes squares. Then I say, "Why don't you put all these things in an order that you like. Don't worry about how it goes together cos we're gonna throw it away at the end."After about twenty minutes, she's put something together that makes sense to her. Then I say, "We are gonna put it together and you can take it home." "You can't do that!" she says. But we do. She just made art for the first time and she's blown away that she did it. Anyone can if they give themselves permission and don't pay attention to the doubting voices, that never seem to go away. 'Thanks for your concern, now shut up and lemme have some fun.'

And what's next for you, Spencer?

Esther and I keep adapting and making our space work for us. When the music industry collapsed we turned the recording studio into an Airbnb. Now we get to meet people from all over the world. And for four years I was a director at Tim's winery, helping to bring products to market and producing events. I didn't have any experience of the wine business when I started but I did know about systems, marketing, event production and bringing people together. Life is a series of chapters and at the moment I'd say I'm in a transitionary period moving from older middle age into elderhood. I still produce art and help other people bring their ideas to fruition but there's been a shift. I'm in great health and there's so much opportunity to have an extremely full life—just in a different way.

May 2020

Mun Wah

"Then Oprah Winfrey decided to do a special show about my work and that's when my whole life changed"

Spencer introduces me to my next and final link and says that while he knows quite a few interesting folks that would make fantastic subjects, his old and very dear friend Mun Wah does work that is particularly relevant to today's times. He is one of the leading trainers, directors, lecturers and authors today around diversity and racism and Spencer says that he has changed thousands, if not hundreds of thousands of people's lives. They've been close friends for thirty-eight years and first bonded over a game of chess. Mun Wah went on to direct award-winning films on racism and some filming was done at Spencer's house. Spencer adds that I will enjoy interviewing Mun Wah as he is 'quite a character, talker and jokester!'

The world is still in the grip of the coronavirus pandemic and to add to the general sense of turbulence, the US has just seen the biggest Black Lives Matter protests to date. There has been a global response to the killing of George Floyd in Minneapolis and the UK has seen its own protests including one in Bristol that hit the headlines when a statue of the slave trader Edward Colston was toppled and rolled down the road before being dumped in the harbour. On its journey it passed the flat where I interviewed Susan W several years ago.

Mun Wah came to international attention in 1995 with his documentary The Color of Fear. Widely described as ground-breaking it was direct, truthful and raw and to date it's been seen by over thirty million people across the world and is required viewing at most colleges in the United States. It continues to inform and influence the debate on racism.

As well as making award-winning documentaries and writing books, Mun Wah is a storyteller and poet and has done a number of TED Talks. He told me how he uses mindful communication to challenge racism, sexism and other injustices in many organisations including Top 500 companies and The Pentagon. We also talked about the traumatic event that changed his life and led him into diversity work.

What was life like when you were growing up, Mun Wah?

There is no way in a thousand years that I could have imagined the life I've had. I was born in the flatlands of Oakland, California and we were whites, blacks, Latinos, and Asians, all living together. It was the 1950s and we were very poor but the thing was that we didn't know we were poor because everyone around us was poor, too. We'd play together and have sleepovers. It was an incredibly warm experience and my mother taught me to value relationships rather than things.

My father worked as a manager in a Chinese restaurant and he dreamed of opening his own place. He saved really hard but unfortunately, just when he started to build his restaurant, Oakland had one of the worst rains in its history. It literally rained for thirty days and thirty nights—Lake Merritt overflowed and there were ducks swimming down the streets. The builders couldn't lay the concrete and my father was running out of money so he took what he had and went to a casino in Reno, Nevada. He won 25,000 dollars and as he was walking out the boss said, "What are you gonna do with all that money?" And he said, "I'm opening up a restaurant in the middle of Oakland. It's gonna be the most beautiful Chinese restaurant ever built." "Oh really," said the casino boss. "We've been trying to get you Chinese people up to Reno. Would you mind giving these special little tickets out to your customers. If you can get them up here, we'll give you a percentage." So that's what he did and it went really well. And then the casino bosses asked if he would organise some buses to take Chinese people out to Reno. They lent my father the money and he set up some bus depots. They made tons of money but the main thing was that they were on some of the most valuable real estate in the entire Bay area. My father eventually became a multi-millionaire and that changed our lives quite a lot.

Despite that, things at home were very dysfunctional as my father was both verbally and physically abusive. He used to beat the shit out of me and I used to think I must be a really bad kid—I always had to say I was sorry. But then my gym teacher picked up what was happening and everything changed. He noticed that I was wearing sweatpants even though it was a really hot day, and he put his arm around me and said, "It's really hard at home, huh?" And I started crying and I told him what was happening. He told the vice principal and they called my father in. After my father had screamed at them, and gone out slamming the door, the vice principal came out and said, "Mun Wah, you're not the problem. It's your father." He was the first adult who had ever made me think it was wrong. When I got home that day, my father told me that I was no longer his son and he was taking me out of his will. "You're on your own," he said and I thought, "OK, well at least I'm done with the beatings."

My two brothers and two sisters were straight-A students at high school but I was getting Cs and Ds. I hated having to memorise things. For me, it took all the joy out of learning. Then one summer I went to stay with my uncle in Utah. He asked what college I was planning to go to when I was older, and when I said I was planning to work for my father instead, he told me I should go to college because I was very smart. He got his sons to help me with things like algebra but the best thing was that before I left, I managed to beat him at chess. And he was a chess master. That really built up my confidence and when I got home I signed up for college prep classes. My brother said, "Are you crazy? You're not that smart," but I went on to be a Junior High School President and by the time I left, I was Student Body President.

And did you go on to college?

I could have gone to the University of California at Berkeley but if I'd done that then my father would have got me to live at home, so I chose a small state college in San Francisco. I lived in Haight-Ashbury and became a hippy. It was the sixties—the time of Martin Luther King and Malcolm X, and we were fighting for civil rights. I learned about social justice and community, and we fought for Black Studies, Asian Studies, Latino Studies and for more teachers of colour. That was the backdrop to my social world and it was magnificent.

What did you do when you graduated?

For about twenty-five years I worked as a special education teacher in San Francisco junior high schools and my classes were predominantly black—these kids were often louder or more physical or more direct than other students but instead of attending to their strengths and getting them to talk, people classified them as having behavior problems. The usual approach was to get them to sit down and be quiet and memorise things. I did things differently and was voted an outstanding teacher but not once in all my years of teaching did any administrator or teacher come into my classroom and ask what I was doing. I was very aware of racism towards black students.

Then everything changed. My mother was murdered by a young African American man who broke into the house. He shot her five times in the head and then went on down the hill to kill another three women. I was deeply traumatised and kept blaming myself for not being there to save her. I contemplated suicide a number of times. Eventually I recognised that the grief would always be with me but I would learn to live with it, and I went into therapy. That led to me becoming a therapist myself.

First I worked in grief therapy. Then I worked with men who were violent and that made me realise how I was afraid of men because of my father. I was referred people of colour and again I was told I was doing phenomenal work. Our models for therapy are based on being white, male, middle class, and heterosexual. But I am a Chinese American man raised in the poor flatlands of Oakland. Where is the interest in what I bring to that—where is the therapy that makes use of people being say, Latino, black, Asian, or international? Not once did any of the people who did the referring ever ask me about my approach. It made me think, "Oh I *see*. I take care of *those* people but what I do and what I have learned in working with them is of no interest to you—of no value to you."

How did you get into making documentaries?

When I first became a therapist I started an Asian men's group in my home. We had food and shared our stories, and we talked about the racism we experienced and our anger. My supervisor at that time didn't know much about people of colour or even issues of race, and after a while he started asking me all these questions and wanting to know more. That was when I said, "The teacher has now become the student," and I went on to do my own work. We were doing these incredible things in the group and The American Psychological Association heard about it. They said they wished there was a film about it so without any film experience, I used my savings to hire some people of colour and I had them film my Asian men's group. It took a year and a half to edit into a documentary called *Stolen Ground*, and it got an honourable mention in the San Francisco Film Festival. It was different and unusual at that time because it had no script. It cost $25,000 and I made that money back in two weeks so I thought film-making was really easy.

Then I started thinking about making *The Color of Fear*, a film with different races all together in one room. I raised about $25,000 and thought it would be just as cheap as the last one. But by the first half day of filming I'd spent all of the money and from that moment on I was in debt. Anyway I did manage to film it and got some incredible footage just by asking, "What is your name and what is your ethnicity?" People of colour simply exploded with conversations that they have with themselves and usually never share. We saw people letting rip with all the passions inside of them, and talking about the effects of racism on their lives and families. Nobody had ever seen a film like this. I set the date for the premiere at a black repertory theatre in Oakland and it sold out within hours. And when it hit the streets people were literally around four blocks in lines. Word spread and people kept having me come to show the film and do diversity work. The audiences that see it are probably around 75% white and I'd hear them say things like, "Oh my God, I had no idea..."

Then Oprah Winfrey decided to do a special show about my work and that's when my whole life changed. Over fifteen million people saw the film at that time and I went on to work in almost every Government agency.

That was in 1995. How are things today?

Things have got much worse under Trump's presidency. His rally call to *Make America Great Again* was meant for white people not people of colour—in fact *especially* not for people of colour. He has inflamed people and given permission to the Ku Klux Klan, Neo-Nazis and other white supremacists to do what they want in this country. Every Republican watched this President lie and condone violence with all his racist rhetoric, and they didn't say a damn word. All these Christians, these Episcopalians, the Evangelicals didn't say a single word. That has complicated and intensified the anguish.

I've noticed in the recent riots that the focus is on the violence not why people are protesting—not on the issues that are happening to blacks. But there is rage and the way it makes the news is when they bring things to a standstill. Martin Luther King said, "Wait has almost always meant *Never*," and Obama said that it requires us to be uncomfortable before we change. How sad that we have to come to it that way.

We could have the ultimate goal that every police chief in this country is a person of colour, and that the next twenty presidents be black. But actually what having had a black president taught me is that it didn't matter who the hell it was—if white people in power don't want change to happen then it's not going to happen. John Boehner was Speaker of the House at the time of President Barack Obama and said he would vote *No* on everything until the next election. And not a single white adult stood up and said, "Who are you working for? This is all about politics." And so for me the anguish just builds up. Is there any fair play? Is there any sense of working together?

There is no company or institution in this country that is not racist and sexist. One study asked top CEOs why they don't hire more women and people of colour, and why they don't promote them. The answers turned out to be mostly about social things and the discomfort of having them around. They said things like "What would we talk about?" and "They wouldn't feel comfortable at our dinners. They might not know how to play golf." And I remember asking a room full of executives, how they keep women and people of colour out. A white guy got up and said, "Piece of cake. First of all we make the qualifications higher for some people but...if they're smart and they get through then we make sure that at least sixty per cent of the test scores come from an interview and are subjective...then we just weed 'em out."

I'll often ask a room of people, "How would you like to get rid of affirmative action overnight?" And everybody says, "Wow, how would you do that?" And I say, "Just make sure that sixty per cent of your hiring group is people of colour and women and gays, and that the sixty per cent of the people who create your policies are people of colour and women and gays. Then you won't need to have affirmative action." Do you know how fast I can get a room to be quiet just by asking those questions? I think that white people are afraid that people of colour and women and minorities will be the majority.

What if when Barack Obama was elected he'd decided to have an all black cabinet. Or if Hillary Clinton had been elected and had an all women cabinet. How do you think white men would have seen that? They would call that reverse racism or reverse sexism. Yet under Ronald Reagan we had an all white male cabinet.

It's easy to say things like, "We must be post-racial because we've had a black president and we have some black millionaires." But the employment of one black man does not mean we are post-racial and the vast majority of black people are not millionaires. I call this unhealthy communication—it's when white people look for the exception and say, "Look, you see it *is* possible."

There are so many ways that people shut these conversations down. I wrote a paper called *21 Ways to Stop a Diversity Conversation* detailing all of the ways that people can stop a person from bringing up diversity issues ever again. And the thing is that they are all nice things to say. Here's an example. Say I want to talk to you about how hard it is to be Chinese. And you simply go to me, "You know Mun Wah, even as I am talking to you today I want you to know that I don't even *see* your colour. To me you are just a human being. And I was taught to love everybody." That's one way, or people will look for exceptions like Obama, or play devil's advocate, or change the topic, or simply say that they've never had that experience themselves.

At a student graduation a few years ago, I asked parents of colour to stand up if they wish they had managers and vice presidents who understand what they go through as people of colour and who would make good use of their skills and what they bring from their culture. They all stood up. I said to the white people there, "This is still missing and you don't even know. And we don't even expect that it will be any different. That's so sad. And until those things are made use of and seen as important we will never be able to get past where we are."

You work with mindful communication. What do you mean by that?

I do believe that change can happen but whites and people of colour need to have real conversations with each other. A survey found out that around ninety per cent of white people don't have any close friends who are of colour. And that those who do, have never asked them about the impact of racism on their lives. The same applies for other issues, like asking what's it like to be gay, or what's it like to be poor. We skip around these things and avoid these questions so I produced a set of flashcards to help people have conversations about racism. It's called *What Stands Between Us* and there are over four hundred questions that people of colour and white people have always wanted to ask one another but were too scared to ask.

In one session I brought six hundred business people together with their vice presidents and presidents who were all people of colour or women. And I had them turn to their vice presidents and presidents and simply say this, "What's good and what's hard about being a person of colour, or a woman, in this company. I would really like to find out. And if you have issues, am I one of those problems?" And the vice presidents asked, "What's it like for you to have a woman in charge? What are your fears and anxieties about it?" or "How many people don't want me in charge because I'm a person of colour?" For two hours, I could not stop them talking and they were saying, "I had no idea…" Some of them were in tears. They had never had those kinds of conversations before.

These things are dying to be shared and are needed for change to take place. But it's not easy—people struggle with hearing the truth. There's a Chinese statue with the saying, *I wanna hear the truth but not too much. I wanna hear the truth but not if it gets emotional. And I wanna hear the truth but not if it's about me.* Would *you* tell the truth if it cost you your job? Would *you* be willing to hear the unfiltered truth and actually reward and promote people for that?

One of my tasks is to get people through the door and into

my workshops and I've learned that what doesn't work is to give long lectures about racism, sexism, homophobia...you name it. You tell people about white privilege and things like that and they get defensive. That's why I changed the titles of my workshops from *Unlearning Racism* and *Looking at White Privilege* to things like *Walking Each Other Home* and *The World is All Around Us*. What we need to teach is curiosity, self-reflection, how to take responsibility, and to be willing to change. Those four things are healthy communication and would you say that the current United States president has any of these attributes?

Most white people who come into my workshops say, "You know, I thought I was going to get attacked. I thought it was all going to be lectures and instead I've made a friend. I've got to know this person. I had no idea their life was like this and I've learned fifteen skills in how to communicate."

A couple of the previous links in the chain were involved in the Ferguson protests. How do you think those protests changed things?

The changes in Ferguson have been phenomenal and they now have a black mayor there. But the changes in Ferguson did not necessarily impact the rest of the country. They happened in a small enclave in a city and did not change the state. There is still a great fear of colour and people who are different. And people are also afraid to talk about whiteness and privilege. That's true here in the US but the footprints of racism are all around the world including Britain.

How optimistic do you feel about change?

I've asked both people of colour and white people whether they think they'll see the end of racism in their lifetime. And everybody has said, "Absolutely not." Then I've asked them what will make this country do anything about racism and the answer is profound but also sad. Change will not happen until people's own children are at stake. It's the same with guns. We talk all the time about how much we hate the shootings and the killings and yet we will not do anything to stop our guns. We love to cry and have prayers and say how sorry we are, and then the next day we're back into our guns again. And so the question is, "Will it take *your* child being shot? Will it take *your* child going to prison? Will it take *your* house to be burned down until you look at all of this and do something?" I don't want to wait till then and so for more than thirty years, I've been having these conversations.

This next generation gives me great hope. I hope they will be unruly, angry and upset any time they see injustice and not see it as an inconvenience. As Al Gore once said, "The inconvenient truth haunts every single generation." I hope this generation will rise to the occasion just as mine did.

And to finish, I want to share a couple of things that I wrote recently. The first is about the courage it takes to make change happen.

> I believe we are all tested. Maybe not in the way we planned or wanted...but, when the time comes, we will either act with courage and goodness or with fear and silence. For each of us deep down knows what is right and what is wrong...and it is at that moment when we are tested that our history is written—to be

> remembered or to be looked back on with regret. It is a choice that we each must make for ourselves and for those not yet born. For each decision we make in life affects everything and everyone from that moment on. Every time we do not speak up, someone always pays a price for our silence...and that same price is also exacted on who we become and who we do not. So, you see, perhaps it is where the road ends, that our path begins.

I wrote this second piece for all those families whose black children and adult children have died so unjustly—and because my mother was murdered. It's about what it does to us and how it feels to survive.

> Sometimes you can't believe it's happening when someone stands up and shares their story. At first it surprises everyone and then you realise that what they're sharing isn't happening to just one person but to lots of other folks who have been silenced or made to doubt themselves. The beauty of when it is finally spoken out loud is that it is so disarmingly honest, so real that you can't even touch it because it is so fragile and so rare. And when it is spoken clearly from the heart it resonates a certain kind of eloquence because throughout history it has always been known by one word. The truth.

June 2020

Conclusions

At the beginning, this chain was nothing more than a fingers-crossed idea and a lot of shapeless speculation. Everything about it was hazy and unknown. All I could do was hope that people would be willing to talk to me, while wondering where they might be and what they might say.

As it happened, things turned out better than I could ever have expected and I discovered with gratitude that people were willing to take part and even seemed to welcome what I was trying to do. Many of them had busy diaries but they were all generous with their time. And as the chain grew link by link like laying railway track, the hazy shapes acquired boundaries and were filled in with real life stories. That track is now laid and I can stand back, look at it in its entirety and make a few observations.

Reflecting on the chain itself, it pleases me to remember that it was not my creation. I may have facilitated its path but it was already there. Those people were and continue to be, connected by invisible threads and a range of affiliations. We're used to describing connections in terms of family relationships—we all know what it means to be a grandmother, niece or stepfather, for example. We can even talk about our connections to people we may never meet such as third cousins twice removed, and with some paper, a pencil and a bit of head scratching we can visualise our relationship. But in the chain the connections are, with one exception (Leonora and John are mother and son), about other ways of relating to one another—friend, teacher, colleague, fellow campaigner, mother's best friend, and best friend's son. And just like family relationships these connections can be articulated, or represented visually. So that Ruth in New York, for example, might not know Spencer in California but she could describe her relationship to him as a friend of her friend's mother's best friend's son. It might take a while for anyone else to work out what that means but it is nonetheless a traceable connection. The idea of six degrees of separation is well-known in popular culture and some academic studies have corroborated its relevance to real life, but those connections are often loose whereas the person-to-person links in the interview chain are robust. They're not just superficial social media connections but meaningful relationships so that any message passed on from one to another would be accompanied by personal touches like 'Good luck with the new project' or 'How's your son?'

In fact some of the relationships are so meaningful as to be life-changing. We've seen how Susan W was encouraged to become an actor by Maria; Helen was inspired to volunteer in a Romanian orphanage by Liz's experiences in India; Liz says she would never have gone to work in India were it not for Gareth's encouragement, and Nicholas was able to rebuild his life with support from the trust fund that Lesley set up in her husband's name to help Rwandans recover from the trauma of the genocide.

I speculated at the beginning about the kinds of things that people would admire in one another and guessed that compassion, wisdom, bravery, and professionalism would show up in various guises. They did. Inevitably everyone's situation was individual and intricate but the characteristic they all shared was a set of values whether social, political or creative that they were willing to stand up for and which they put to use in their work. Several interviewees—particularly Kirsti, Ruth, Susan T, John and Leonora—talked about their upbringing and how their parents' moral values had affected their own values and the decisions they had made. It was heartening to meet the younger interviewees at the start of the chain who were so full of energy for various causes and cared about making a better world. And many of the older interviewees had been through hard times but still maintained their essential belief in the potential for social change. One interviewee whilst holding firm to her core beliefs felt that she had developed and changed quite a bit since I did the interview, as young people are inclined to do. So she asked me to anonymise the interview, which of course I did.

The idea of getting the interviewees to pave the path turned out to have unexpected benefits. If I'd chosen a group of interviewees myself then it's likely I'd have ended up exploring things that I already knew something about—the known knowns—or things that I didn't know much about but was nonetheless aware of—the known unknowns. But by relinquishing control I found myself talking to people I would never have come across, and through them the project touched on a number of issues that were completely new to me—the unknown unknowns. Before talking to John I knew nothing about the plight of child soldiers in Central Africa, and it was only through my conversation with Helen that I learned the extent of the neglect in the Romanian orphanages in the 1990s. These and many of the other stories are powerful and unforgettable.

As for the referral process, people seemed pleased to be asked and several said that they were honoured to be chosen. It was a way for them to unequivocally and publicly acknowledge their value to one another. Several also commented that they found the interview itself, useful—a way to reflect on their life so far.

In the introduction to Ruth's interview I referred to having learned about my own listening skills and the fact that by listening to the recording of the interview I discovered how much I missed the first time around. This, despite being convinced that I had listened attentively. It was an unplanned exercise in listening but I'd recommend it to anyone. Try recording a conversation, having first got your conversational partner's permission, and ideally choose a topic that they feel strongly about. Later, you can listen to the recording and ask yourself whether you got the full implications of what they were saying. Why did they choose to tell you those particular things and why were they important? Generous listening is a buzzphrase. It's about being genuinely curious to hear what the other person says—to keep the conversation going with a question that encourages exploration, or by giving a reassuring nod. And to attempt to understand their perspective rather than jumping in with our own judgements or missing much of what they say because we're thinking about our response.

My ideas about increasing understanding and promoting empathy were initially quite loose but they grew during this project and became core elements. And so it was serendipitous that the final interview should be with Mun Wah who had so much to say about healthy communication and the importance of trying to see things from the other person's point of view, often called perspective-taking. I'd spotted the Alice in Wonderland connection between Kirsti the first interviewee and Spencer the nineteenth and commented on this. But with Mun Wah things really did come full circle. The project was about sharing stories and the final story was itself about sharing stories.

Mun Wah, Mike, Ruth, Mala, Susan T, Gareth and others talked about the need to challenge prejudice, ignorance and polarisation and to plant the seeds of acceptance, knowledge and nuance. Lack of exposure to other people's lives can feed negative reactions and it's relevant that a nationwide survey by the think tank *British Future* and the advocacy group *HOPE not hate* found that anti-Muslim prejudice was strongest in areas with relatively small Muslim populations. There are now countless imaginative and diverse projects around the world that aim to help people understand one another's perspectives better and I've included in an appendix a small selection of resources that I've found useful and inspirational.

Making an effort to understand another person's situation will often result in a better relationship, with improvements in kindness, respect, honesty and equality. But it would, of course, be misleading and naive to suggest that perspective-taking offers a solution to all of the problems that blight human relationships. Whilst, the people in this chain have all inspired others, I could equally well have collected stories from people who are not widely admired. Those who have committed crimes, for example and do not—yet—have stories of redemption and personal growth. Hearing those kinds of stories is a different and potentially valuable step in understanding what motivates and affects other members of society but it can be difficult to put ourselves in another person's shoes, particularly if that other person has values that differ significantly from our own. It's easy to get carried away with the general positivity that surrounds the idea of perspective-taking but it needs to be handled with care or it could result in entrenched stereotyping and polarisation, quite the opposite of what is intended.

And of course, while we might long for a solution to some of the world's most pressing problems, it's obvious that empathy alone, is not going to provide it. We may feel better about ourselves for caring but if we simply express some empathy and move on, then little has changed. Ruth pointed out with the cool objectivity that comes from years of political experience, that the challenge is to shift people from caring and service, towards policy advocacy. That's how social change comes about—by thinking as well as feeling, and by understanding the structures that underpin complex issues like refugee crises, homelessness and environmental degradation.

These provisos are important but I remain keen on sharing stories and this project has only sharpened that enthusiasm. We cannot all be international aid workers or politicians but we can subscribe to Theodore Zeldin's idea that interaction between people is the motor of change. Any of us can choose to do things that bring us into contact with people, either real or virtual, that we might not ordinarily encounter—volunteering, talking to our neighbours, taking part in community events, visiting museums that document people's experiences, and broadening our social circle by introducing our friends to one another and encouraging them to do the same. Some of my most stimulating friendships are a result of meeting friends of friends who inhabit quite different worlds from my own. And when travelling I nearly always choose Airbnbs over faceless hotels—it's a great way to get the local angle.

Not everyone wants to have a conversation. Some people find it intrusive but if people are of a mind to chat then showing an interest helps them to feel that their opinions and experiences are valued. And if someone makes the effort to understand you, then pass that on and make the effort to understand someone else. You never know what you might learn.

Appendix 1

Resources related to the interviewees

Some of the interviewees have websites, have written books or directed me to further reading. You can find more information here:

Kirsti has a website with photos and details about her work—www.kirstidavies.com

Lesley has written two books about her experiences in Rwanda:

The Colour of Darkness: A Personal Story of Tragedy and Hope in Rwanda. Lesley Bilinda. Hodder Christian Paperbacks, 1996.

With What Remains: A Woman's Search for Truth in the Country that Murdered Her Husband. Lesley Bilinda. Hodder & Stoughton, 2006.

Nicholas is helping to rebuild lives through the Ikirezi Natural Products company which maximises profits to small farmers, holistically transforms communities and strengthens agri-business in Rwanda—www.ikirezi.com

Becca set up Thistle Farms a community of healing and hope for women survivors of trafficking, prostitution, and addiction—thistlefarms.org.

Love Welcomes is a UK-based not-for-profit enterprise set up in partnership with Thistle Farms, that helps refugee women from Syria begin to stitch their lives back together. They weave welcome doormats from the life vests and blankets that they received when they landed on the shores of Europe, exhausted and frightened—www.lovewelcomes.org

Mike mentioned *Bravely*, a St. Louis-based apparel company run by women recovering from sexual exploitation and addiction—wearbravely.org

Together with her family, **Susan T** set up the Adina Talve-Goodman Fellowship in memory of her daughter. This fellowship offers a year-long mentorship on the craft of fiction writing with One Story magazine, and is given to 'an emerging writer whose work speaks to issues and experiences related to inhabiting bodies of difference.'

John directed me towards *To Stop a Warlord*—set in central Africa it's an account of the *Bridgeway Foundation*'s collaborative attempts to bring an end to LRA atrocities. He said, "It's a hard read because it's set in war torn areas and the stories are heart-wrenching. I've had some friends say they read the first chapter and just couldn't go on. I understand that and people need to make good decisions for themselves about what they can cope with, but it's also exhilarating and the best example of what we've done." I read it in a couple of sittings and was gripped. In places it was hard to take in the horror of the atrocities but I wholeheartedly recommend it as an account of what courageous, committed, visionary people can do to turn things around and bring hope out of darkness—To Stop a Warlord: My Story of Justice, Grace, and the Fight for Peace. Shannon Sedgwick Davis. Random House, 2019.

The slogan of **Tim's** California-based winery is 'At Mendocino Wine Company we believe in leaving the world better than we found it'—mendocinowineco.com

More about **Spencer's** music career at www.spencerbrewer.com and photos of his art work at—www.harmonygaits.com

Details of **Mun Wah's** books, films and training—www.stirfryseminars.com

Appendix 2

A selection of perspective-taking and empathy-boosting projects that I've found useful:

- The Migration Museum. This small museum in South London focuses on the movement of people to and from Britain across the ages and how that has made us who we are as individuals and as a nation. It offers a varied programme of exhibitions, events and education workshops and the website has lots of resources including personal stories. www.migrationmuseum.org

- Empathy Museum. A series of roaming art installations designed to help people develop empathy and change their views about global issues like prejudice, conflict and inequality. A Mile in My Shoes invites visitors to put on a pair of shoes and walk in them whilst listening to their owner's story on headphones. The stories are diverse and encompass many aspects of life. I did this when the installation came to my city and heard a mother's affecting account of her daughter's severe depression. Many of the stories are available on the website. www.empathymuseum.com

- Refugee Week. A UK-wide festival and also a growing global movement, that celebrates the contribution, creativity and resilience of refugees. It takes place each June and promotes positive encounters between communities, helping them to connect and learn from one another. refugeeweek.org.uk

- The Human Library. Originating in Denmark this is now a global movement that aims to challenge stereotyping and prejudice. Volunteers (human books) attend festivals and other events to have conversations and answer questions about their particular life experience usually based around topics such as ethnicity, mental health, disabilities, social status, occupation or religion. www.humanlibrary.org and Human Library UK has a Facebook page.

- Tenx9. Storytelling events in various locations around the world where nine people have up to ten minutes each to tell a true story from their own life based around a particular theme. I stumbled on this completely by accident on a visit to Adelaide and had a thoroughly memorable evening—some of the stories were moving and others were hilarious. They were all thought-provoking. Even if you can't get to a physical meeting you can listen to the podcast. The website has dozens of stories available for download. www.tenx9.com

- International Coalition of Sites of Conscience. A worldwide network of Sites of Conscience (historic sites, place-based museums or memorials that provide safe places to remember and to enable their visitors to make connections between past traumatic events and related contemporary human rights issues). There are over 300 members in 65 countries engaged in diverse projects many of which involve people sharing their stories and experiences in order to foster trust and understanding. www.sitesofconscience.org.

- The Oxford Muse. Set up by the philosopher Theodore Zeldin, this is a movement which encourages conversations between people who do not know one another. His view is that mixing people up as much as possible is the best way to recognise what they have in common. The website has innovative ideas for improving personal, professional and intercultural relationships. www.oxfordmuse.com

- United Nations Virtual Reality Series. Short films that aim to push the bounds of empathy by showing the everyday realities of some of the world's most vulnerable people. They are designed to be viewed through virtual reality headsets but can also be watched online. unvr.sdgactioncampaign.org

Acknowledgements

There's no doubt here—I'm greatly indebted to the twenty people who trusted me, gave their time so generously and were willing to share their stories even when they were painful. Kirsti deserves a special thank you as she was the first and that required making a leap of faith.

Some interviewees had assistants who managed their diaries, and I had a number of exchanges with them when arranging the interviews. Thank you to Marlei, Laura, Erin and Ellen who were unfailingly efficient and friendly.

I'm grateful for the support and interest of friends and family especially Mike Poppleton, Will Mawhood, Liberty York, Henry Baroche, Mima Farley-Rose, Matt Aitken, Anne Robin, and Gimma Macpherson whose encouraging words helped when I got stuck. Jo Dalton has done a great job on the cover as she did with my previous book, and Robert Peett my editor and publisher brings wisdom and integrity to all that he does.

Acknowledgements

Photo credits

Kirsti: Kirsti on a Spicy Ricksaw at Kew Gardens

Megan: Mongolian Gers (attribution - Annawhitney, CC BY-SA 4.0 https://creativecommons.org/licenses/by-sa/4.0, via Wikimedia Commons) Link is https://commons.wikimedia.org/wiki/File:Two_Mongolian_Gers.jpg

Becca: Erica Baker - link https://brandfolder.com/thistle-farms

Ruth: Jeff Zorbedian

Lynn: Mike Poppleton